Excellent English 1
Language Skills for Success

Susannah MacKay
Kristin D. Sherman

Jan Forstrom
Marta Pitt
Shirley Velasco

Workbook by Janet Podnecky

 **McGraw-Hill**

Excellent English Workbook 1

ISBN 13: 978-0-07-719388-1
ISBN 10: 0-07-719388-1
1 2 3 4 5 6 7 8 9 10 QPD 11 10 09 08 07

Developmental editor: Regina Velázquez
Cover designer: Witz End Design
Interior designer: NETS

Illustrators: Punto 5, Silvia Plata, Ismael Vázquez Sánchez and Carlos Mendoza Alemán

Other Photos: Edgewater Pictures, pp. 16, 30, 44, 58, 72, 86, 100, 128, 142, 156, and 170

Cover photo:
    Hand: Getty
    Vet: Corbis
    Family with sold sign: Corbis
    Chef: Corbis
    Architect: Corbis
    Pix in Hand: MMH

To the Teacher

PROGRAM OVERVIEW

> **Excellent English: Language Skills for Success** equips students with the grammar and skills they need to access community resources while developing the foundation for long-term career and academic success.

Excellent English is a four-level, grammar-oriented series for English learners featuring a *Grammar Picture Dictionary* approach to vocabulary building and grammar acquisition. An accessible and predictable sequence of lessons in each unit systematically builds language and math skills around life-skill topics. *Excellent English* is tightly correlated to all of the major standards for adult instruction.

- CASAS (the Comprehensive Adult Student Assessment Systems)

- Los Angeles Unified School District's Competency-Based Education (CBE) Course Outlines

- Florida Adult ESOL Syllabi

- EFF (Equipped for the Future) Content Standards

- SCANS (Secretary's Commission on Achieving Necessary Skills)

The *Excellent English* Workbook with Audio CD is an essential companion to the Student Book. Each workbook unit provides 14 pages of supplementary practice for its corresponding Student Book unit. The Workbook provides students with further practice with the grammar, vocabulary, listening, reading, writing, and life-skill competencies taught in the Student Book. It offers application lessons that cover competencies in addition to those that are covered in the Student Book.

Features

- **Family Connection** and **Community Connection** lessons provide practice with additional competencies related to the topic of each Student Book unit.

- **Career Connection** lessons build off the Career Connection photo story in the Student Book and address additional work-related competencies.

- **Technology Connection** lessons introduce students to technology objectives as they are used in everyday life, such as using an ATM, email, or a computer calendar.

- **Culture and Communication** activities introduce culturally appropriate communication strategies, such as asking for clarification or repetition.

- **Real-Life Lessons** take learning beyond the classroom as students use new language skills to gather information about their own community through interviews and research.

- **Practice tests** in every unit, complete with CASAS-type listening tasks from the Workbook CD, encourage students to test their skills in a low stakes environment.

- An **Audio CD**—packaged with each Workbook— includes recorded passages for the Listening and Conversation and Culture and Communication lessons, as well as for the practice tests.

Contents

Pre-Unit

Letters and Numbers 2
Classroom Directions 4
Grammar: Parts of Speech 5

Unit 1

ALL ABOUT YOU

Lesson 1 6
Lesson 2 7
Lesson 3 8
Culture and Communication—*Greetings* 9
Lesson 4 10
Lesson 5 11
Family Connection—*Activities at the Library* 12
Community Connection—*Write a Letter* 14
Career Connection—*Make Copies* 16
Technology Connection: Email Addresses 17
Practice Test 18

Unit 2

PEOPLE

Lesson 1 20
Lesson 2 21
Lesson 3 22
Culture and Communication—*Describe People* 23
Lesson 4 24
Lesson 5 25
Family Connection—*Emergency Contacts* 26
Community Connection—*Emergency Numbers* 28
Career Connection—*People at Work* 30
Technology Connection: When to Use a Cell Phone 31
Practice Test 32

Unit 3

AT SCHOOL

Lesson 1 34
Lesson 2 35
Lesson 3 36
Culture and Communication—*Ask Questions at the Library* ... 37
Lesson 4 38
Lesson 5 39
Family Connection—*Open House at School* 40
Community Connection—*Read a Building Directory* 42
Career Connection—*Ask for Office Supplies* 44
Technology Connection: Use Email to Ask for Help 45
Practice Test 46

Unit 4

IT'S ABOUT TIME!

Lesson 1 48
Lesson 2 49
Lesson 3 50
Culture and Communication—*Talk About the Weather* 51
Lesson 4 52
Lesson 5 53
Family Connection—*Extreme Weather* 54
Community Connection—*Weather Forecast* 56
Career Connection—*Computer Calendars* 58
Technology Connection: Set an Event on a Computer Calendar 59
Practice Test 60

Unit 5

IN THE COMMUNITY

Lesson 1 62
Lesson 2 63
Lesson 3 64
Culture and Communication—*Ask for More Information* 65
Lesson 4 66
Lesson 5 67
Family Connection—*Emergencies* 68
Community Connection—*Get a Driver's License* 70
Career Connection—*Websites* 72
Technology Connection: Use Links 73
Practice Test 74

Unit 6

SHOPPING

Lesson 1 76
Lesson 2 77
Lesson 3 78
Culture and Communication—*Give Feedback* 79
Lesson 4 80
Lesson 5 81
Family Connection—*Cash or Credit?* 82
Community Connection—*Describe Clothing* 84
Career Connection—*Write Checks* 86
Technology Connection: Use an ATM 87
Practice Test 88

Unit 7

DAILY ROUTINES

Lesson 1 90
Lesson 2 91
Lesson 3 92
Culture and Communication—*Talk about Daily Activities* 93
Lesson 4 94
Lesson 5 95
Family Connection—*Help Your Child in School*............................... 96
Community Connection—*Bus Schedules* 98
Career Connection—*Time-Keeping Forms*..................................... 100
Technology Connection: Use a Time Clock 101
Practice Test 102

Unit 8

LET'S EAT!

Lesson 1 104
Lesson 2 105
Lesson 3 106
Culture and Communication—*Would You Like . . . ?*.......................107
Lesson 4 108
Lesson 5 109
Family Connection—*Healthy Eating*.. 110
Community Connection—*Weights and Measures*............................ 112
Career Connection—*Plan Food and Drinks* 114
Technology Connection: Scales 115
Practice Test 116

Unit 9

SKILLS AND WORK

Lesson 1 118
Lesson 2 119
Lesson 3 120
Culture and Communication—*Talk about Your Skills*......................121
Lesson 4 122
Lesson 5 123
Family Connection—*Jobs*... 124
Community Connection—*Apply for a Job*....................................... 126
Career Connection—*Self-Assessment Forms* 128
Technology Connection: How to Use a Computer Spell Check....................... 129
Practice Test 130

Unit 10

TAKING A TRIP

Lesson 1 132
Lesson 2 133
Lesson 3 134
Culture and Communication—*Call to Say You're Late* 135
Lesson 4 136
Lesson 5 137
Family Connection—*Pay the Fare* 138
Community Connection—*Subway Map* 140
Career Connection—*Online Traffic Reports* 142
Technology Connection: Use an Online Map 143
Practice Test 144

Unit 11

HEALTH MATTERS

Lesson 1 146
Lesson 2 147
Lesson 3 148
Culture and Communication—*Talk about How You Feel* 149
Lesson 4 150
Lesson 5 151
Family Connection—*Call for a Medical Appointment* 152
Community Connection—*Injuries* 154
Career Connection—*Read Insurance Forms* 156
Technology Connection: Get Health Insurance Information 157
Practice Test 158

Unit 12

PLANNING AHEAD

Lesson 1 160
Lesson 2 161
Lesson 3 162
Culture and Communication—*Talk about Your Plans* 163
Lesson 4 164
Lesson 5 165
Family Connection—*Things That Use Electricity* 166
Community Connection—*Shop for Appliances* 168
Career Connection—*Career and Personal Goals* 170
Technology Connection: Online Banking 171
Practice Test 172

Student Book/Workbook Correlation Table 174

Correlation Charts

Unit 1 ALL ABOUT YOU

LCPs	EE Book 1	LAUSD	EE Book 1	CASAS	EE Book 1
2.15.03 Rewrite a list of names in alphabetical order.	SB: 6, 7, 9, 11, 15, 17, 19 WB: 6, 7, 11, 18	1. Identify first, middle, and last names and state name of self and others.	SB: 6, 7, 9, 11, 15, 16, 17, 18,19 WB: 6, 7, 11, 15, 18	0.2.1 Respond appropriately to common personal information questions.	SB: 6, 7, 9, 11, 15, 17, 19 WB: 6, 7, 11, 18
2.15.05 Fill out various forms. 2.01.03 Complete a job application form.	SB: 16, 20 WB: 6, 7, 19	2. Identify simple addresses, including abbreviations, compass directions, city, state and country.	SB: 6, 16, 17, 19 WB: 6, 7	0.2.2 Complete a personal information form.	SB: 6, 16, 17, 19 WB: 6, 7
3.15.10 Use a bilingual and/or picture dictionary.	SB: 6 WB: 12	4. Distinguish among various personal information numbers, including telephone, zip code, social security and date of birth.	SB: 6, 7, 10, 16, 17, 19 WB: 8, 11	0.2.3 Interpret or write a personal note, invitation, or letter.	SB: 18, 19 WB: 11, 15, 17
2.16.01 Use subject pronouns (*I, you, he, she, it we, they*).	SB: 6, 7, 8, 9, 12, 13 WB: 6, 7, 10, 12	6. Identify family members, marital status and gender.	SB: 6, 14, 17, 18, 19, 28, 31, 33, 39 WB: 6, 7, 10, 19, 24, 25, 26	4.1.8 Identify common occupations and the skills and education required for them.	SB: 6, 12, 13, 14, 17, 18, 21 WB: 10, 11, 14
2.15.07 Apply word attack skills necessary for reading fluency. (Include phonemic awareness, phonics, fluency, sight words, and spelling.)	SB: 7, 9, 21 WB: 14, 18, 19	7. Interpret and fill out a simple form with basic personal information.	SB: 16, 18, 20 WB: 6, 7, 19	0.1.2 Identify or use appropriate language for informational purposes (e.g., to identify, describe, ask for information, state needs, command, agree or disagree, ask permission).	SB: 6, 7, 8, 9 WB: 6, 7, 9, 14
2.05.01 Use appropriate language for interpersonal communication in formal and informal situations (greetings, introductions, thanks, expressing pleasure, regrets, and farewells).	SB: 11, 20, 21 WB: 6, 9, 18	1. Use simple present tense with: a. the verb *be* in communication about personal information, occupations, feelings, location, names, and descriptions of objects and people, time, and the weather c. the first, second, and third person verb forms of the common verbs used for regularly occurring events (e.g., *I work on Mondays.*)	SB: 6, 21 WB: 12	0.1.4 Identify or use appropriate language in general social situations (e.g., to greet, introduce, thank, apologize, compliment, express pleasure or regret).	SB: 11, 20, 21 WB: 6, 9, 18
2.01.01 Identify job and workplaces of various occupations.	SB: 6, 12, 13, 14, 17, 18, 21 WB: 10, 11, 14	60. Scan for specific information in simple reading material.	SB: 18 WB: 16		
2.16.09 Use articles (*a, an, the*). 3.16.05 Use definite (*the*) and indefinite (*a, an*) articles.	SB: 13, 21 WB: 10, 18	10. Use determiners appropriately. a. articles: *a, an, the*	SB: 13, 21 WB: 10, 18		
		50. Identify common occupations.	SB: 6, 12, 13, 14, 17, 18, 21 WB: 10, 11, 14		
		8. Address an envelope.	SB: 23		
		5. Identify country of origin.	SB: 7, 9, 10, 11, 15, 18, 19 WB: 6, 11, 14		

Unit 2 PEOPLE

LCPs	EE Book 1	LAUSD	EE Book 1	CASAS	EE Book 1
2.06.02 Take written telephone messages. 3.06.02 Use appropriate telephone greetings, leave an oral message, and take a written message.	SB: 32, 33 WB: 27, 28, 29	19. Identify self and ask to speak with someone on the telephone.	SB: 32, 33 WB: 27, 28, 29	2.1.7 Take and interpret telephone messages, leave messages on answering machines, and interpret recorded messages. 2.1.8 Use the telephone to make and receive routine personal and business calls.	SB: 32, 33 WB: 27, 28, 29
2.06.01 Demonstrate ability to use different types of telephones to make local, long distance, collect, and person-to-person calls. 3.06.02 Use appropriate telephone greetings, leave an oral message, and take a written message.	SB: 32, 33 WB: 27, 28, 29	20. Respond appropriately to a telephone call (e.g., *Hold on please. He isn't here right now.*).	SB: 32, 33 WB: 27, 28, 29	2.1.7 Take and interpret telephone messages, leave messages on answering machines, and interpret recorded messages.	SB: 32, 33 WB: 27, 28, 29
2.14.01 Identify family members and their relationships. 3.14.01 Identify family relationships.	SB: 28, 31, 33, 39 WB: 24, 25, 26	16. Use the following question types: a. *Yes/No* questions and answers	SB: 22, 23, 24, 25, 26, 27 WB: 20, 30	0.1.4 Identify or use appropriate language in general social situations (e.g., to greet, introduce, thank, apologize, compliment, express pleasure or regret). 0.2.4 Converse about daily and leisure activities and personal interests.	SB: 22, 23, 24, 25 WB: 20, 21, 22, 23, 24, 25
2.16.07 Use descriptive adjectives. 3.16.03 Use adjectives: – descriptive – possessive – demonstrative	SB: 22, 23, 24, 25, 26, 27, 31, 34, 35 WB: 21	9. Use nouns appropriately. c. possessive forms (e.g., *John's book*)	SB: 30, 37 WB: 24, 25, 27, 32	2.6.1 Interpret information about recreational and entertainment facilities and activities.	SB: 22, 23, 24, 25, 26, 27 WB: 20, 30
2.16.10 Use possessive adjectives (*my, your, his, her, our, their*). 3.16.03 Use adjectives: – descriptive – possessive – demonstrative	SB: 22, 23, 24, 25, 26, 28, 29, 35, 36 WB: 22, 32	9. Use nouns appropriately. b. singular and plural nouns	SB: 30, 37 WB: 24, 25, 27, 32	2.7.6 Interpret materials related to the arts, such as fine art, music, drama, and film.	SB: 22, 23, 24, 27, 31, 34, 35, 36 WB: 21
2.15.06 Write sentences on a familiar topic using appropriate punctuation.	SB: 25, 29, 36 WB: 20, 21, 22, 24	10. Use determiners appropriately. c. possessive adjectives: *my, your, his, her, its, our, your (plural), their*	SB: 22, 23, 24, 25, 26, 28, 29, 35, 36 WB: 22, 32		
		12. Use adjectives appropriately. a. *be* + adjective (e.g., *She's happy.*)	SB: 22, 23, 24, 27, 31, 34, 35, 36 WB: 21		

Unit 3 AT SCHOOL

LCPs	EE Book 1	LAUSD	EE Book 1	CASAS	EE Book 1
2.16.08 Use prepositions.	SB: 44, 45, 51, 53 WB: 36, 38, 39, 40, 42, 44	14. Use simple prepositions. a. of place: *in, on, at, next to, across, from,* etc. d. of origin: *from*	SB: 44, 45, 51, 53 WB: 36, 38, 39, 40, 42, 44	6.1.3 Multiply whole numbers.	SB: 40
2.09.01 Interpret transportation signs using sight words and symbols. 2.09.02 Follow directions found on public buildings and directories.	SB: 46, 48 WB: 38, 39, 40, 42, 43, 46	15. Identify classroom items.	SB: 38, 40, 41 WB: 34, 35	2.1.8 Use the telephone to make and receive routine personal and business calls. 2.5.6 Use library services.	SB: 43 WB: 36, 37, 44
2.09.04 Interpret maps related to driving and travel needs.	SB: 45, 49 WB: 40, 42, 44, 46, 47	17. Ask and answer questions about school locations.	SB: 39, 42, 49 WB: 39, 40, 42, 47	2.2.1 Ask for, give, follow, or clarify directions.	SB: 44, 45 WB: 37, 39, 42, 43, 47
3.16.07 Use information questions.	SB: 40, 41, 43, 51 WB: 36, 37, 44, 45, 46, 47	23. Interpret and use a simple map. a. Identify right and left with respect to locations. (e.g., *The library is on the right.*) b. Ask and answer questions about location of places in the community.	SB: 47, 48, 50 WB: 41	2.5.5 Locate and use educational services in the community, including interpreting and writing school-related communications.	SB: 46, 47 WB: 36, 37, 38, 43
				2.5.4 Read, interpret, and follow directions found on public signs and building.	SB: 48, 49 WB: 38, 39, 40, 41, 42, 43

Unit 4 IT'S ABOUT TIME!

LCPs	EE Book 1	LAUSD	EE Book 1	CASAS	EE Book 1
2.13.01 Access information about weather conditions.	SB: 54, 55, 56, 57, 66, 69 WB: 48, 49, 50, 51, 54, 55, 60, 61	25. Ask for and tell time on a digital clock and a clock with hands.	SB: 60, 63 WB: 52, 60, 61	2.3.2 Identify the months of the year and the days of the week.	SB: 56, 57, 62, 64, 65, 69 WB: 52, 56, 58, 59, 60, 61
2.13.02 Respond appropriately to weather emergencies. 3.13.01 Describe various weather conditions and respond appropriately to weather emergencies.	SB: 58 WB: 55, 57	26. Identify and state day, date and month on a basic calendar. 27. Interpret a simple appointment card with date and time.	SB: 56, 57, 62, 64, 65, 69 WB: 52, 56, 58, 59, 60, 61	2.3.3 Interpret information about weather conditions. 5.7.3 Interpret information about earth-related sciences.	SB: 54, 55, 56, 57, 66, 69 WB: 48, 49, 50, 51, 54, 55, 60, 61
3.08.02 Interpret clock time.	SB: 60, 63 WB: 52, 60, 61	28. Ask about and describe the weather and seasons.	SB: 54, 55, 56, 57, 59, 66 WB: 48, 49, 50, 51, 52, 54, 55, 60	2.3.1 Interpret clock time.	SB: 60, 63 WB: 52, 60, 61
2.08.03 Write days of the week and months of the year using words, abbreviations and numerical forms. 3.08.03 Demonstrate use of a calendar by identifying days of the week and months of the year along with the ability to write date in numerical form.	SB: 56, 57, 62, 64, 65, 69 WB: 49, 56, 58, 59, 60, 61	29. Interpret temperatures using the Fahrenheit scale.	SB: 54, 58 WB: 50	1.1.5 Interpret temperatures.	SB: 54, 58 WB: 50
2.08.02 Recognize culturally appropriate concepts of time for school, work, and social activities.	SB: 64, 65 WB: 52, 53, 58, 59	40. Identify national holidays.	SB: 62, 68, 69 WB: 52, 53, 60, 61	2.7.1 Interpret information about holidays.	SB: 62, 68, 69 WB: 52, 53, 60, 61
2.08.01 Associate cardinal and ordinal numbers with quantities and sequencing. 3.08.01 Identify and use ordinal and cardinal numbers.	SB: 61, 62, 63 WB: 53	3. Identify ages and birth dates, using both cardinal and ordinal numbers.	SB: 61, 62, 63 WB: 53	0.2.3 Interpret or write a personal note, invitation, or letter.	SB: 66, 67 WB: 49, 55, 57, 59
3.16.02 Use common verbs (affirmative, negative, yes/no questions, short answers, "wh" questions): – to be – present continuous – simple present tense – future will, "going to" – simple past – modals (present)	SB: 61, 62, 63, 64, 65, 66, 69 WB: 48, 51, 52, 55, 59	12. Use adjectives appropriately. a. be + adjective (e.g., She's happy.) b. adjective + noun (e.g., He's wearing a red shirt.)	SB: 56, 59, 62, 67 WB: 49, 50, 52, 53, 55	2.5.5 Locate and use educational services in the community, including interpreting and writing school-related communications.	SB: 64, 65 WB: 49, 55, 57, 58
2.16.02 Use regular and irregular verbs (affirmative, negative, yes/no questions, short answers, "wh" questions): – present continuous – to be (present) – simple present – simple past – simple future 3.16.03 Use adjectives: – descriptive – possessive – demonstrative	SB: 56, 57, 59, 69 WB: 50, 51, 53, 55	14. Use simple prepositions. c. of time: in, on, at	SB: 60, 62, 63, 67, 69 WB: 48, 49, 50, 51, 52, 53, 60		

Unit 5 IN THE COMMUNITY

LCPs	EE Book 1	LAUSD	EE Book 1	CASAS	EE Book 1
2.09.01 Interpret transportation signs using sight words and symbols. 3.09.04 Read and understand traffic signs.	SB: 76, 78 WB: 70	22. Identify common places in the community.	SB: 70, 71 WB: 63, 64, 65	2.2.2 Recognize and use signs related to transportation.	SB: 76, 78 WB: 66, 70, 74
2.09.02 Follow directions found on public buildings and directories. 3.09.03 Demonstrate ability to read a map, locate places, follow simple instructions related to geographical directions (*N, S, E, W*; right, left).	SB: 71, 72, 73, 75, 77, 79, 80, 81, 84 WB: 63, 66, 67, 68, 74, 75	23. Interpret and use a simple map. a. Identify right and left with respect to locations. (e.g., *The library is on the right.*) b. Ask and answer questions about location of places in the community.	SB: 73, 74, 79, 80, 81 WB: 62, 66, 75	2.5.3 Locate medical and health facilities in the community. 2.6.1 Interpret information about recreational and entertainment facilities and activities.	SB: 70, 71, 72, 73, 74, 75 WB: 63, 64
2.09.03 Compare safe driving practices. 3.09.06 Identify safe driving practices (seat belts, child safety restraints).	SB: 76, 78 WB: 70	14. Use simple prepositions. a. of place: *in, on, at, next to, across, from,* etc.	SB: 70, 71 WB: 63, 64, 65, 66, 74	2.2.1 Ask for, give, follow, or clarify directions. 2.2.2 Recognize and use signs related to transportation.	SB: 70, 71, 72, 75, 76, 77, 78, 79, 80 WB: 60, 66, 67, 68, 74, 75
2.09.04 Interpret maps related to driving and travel needs. 3.09.03 Demonstrate ability to read a map, locate places, follow simple instructions related to geographical directions (*N, S, E, W*; right, left).	SB: 73, 74, 79, 80, 81 WB: 62, 66, 75	5. Express and respond appropriately to affirmative and negative commands (e.g., *Press firmly. Look out! Don't smoke.*).	SB: 76, 77, 85 WB: 65, 67, 70, 75	2.5.1 Locate and utilize services of agencies that provide emergency help. 2.6.2 Locate information in TV, movie, and other recreational listings.	SB: 70, 72, 73, 75, 82 WB: 63, 64
2.12.01 Locate government agencies.	SB: 71, 73, 74 WB: 62, 65, 66, 70, 71	42. Identify simple highway and traffic signs.	SB: 76, 78 WB: 70	2.2.5 Use maps relating to travel needs.	SB: 71, 72, 73, 75, 77, 79, 80, 81, 84 WB: 63, 66, 67, 68, 74, 75
2.12.02 Locate community service agencies. 3.12.01 Identify places in the community and describe public services.	SB: 70, 71, 73, 74, 75, 82, 83, 85 WB: 63, 64	12. Use adjectives appropriately. a. *be* + adjective (e.g., *She's happy.*) b. adjective + noun (e.g., *He's wearing a red shirt.*)	SB: 71, 72, 75, 76, 82, 83 WB: 63, 65, 72, 73		
2.12.03 Access postal services. 3.12.02 Demonstrate ability to purchase stamps, address letters and packages, and mail a letter or package.	SB: 70, 74, 75 WB: 65				
2.16.08 Use prepositions. 3.16.04 Use prepositions.	SB: 70, 71 WB: 63, 64, 65, 66, 74				

Unit 6 SHOPPING

LCPs	EE Book 1	LAUSD	EE Book 1	CASAS	EE Book 1
2.08.04 Match U.S. currency and prices.	SB: 92, 93, 94, 95, 96, 98, 100 WB: 80, 81, 82, 85, 87, 88, 89	30. Use U.S. money. a. Identify U.S. coins and bills. b. Make simple change with U.S. coins and bills.	SB: 92, 96, 97, 100, 101 WB: 81, 82, 87, 89	1.1.6 Count, convert, and use coins and currency, and recognize symbols such as ($) and (.). 1.8.1 Demonstrate the use of savings and checking accounts, including using an ATM.	SB: 92, 93, 94, 95, 96, 98, 100 WB: 80, 81, 82, 85, 87, 88, 89
2.08.07 Write a check and/or money order.	SB: 96, 97, 101 WB: 82, 83, 86, 89	31. Ask for and give prices of common items.	SB: 92, 93, 94, 95, 96, 98, 99, 100, 101 WB: 80, 83, 84, 85, 88, 89	1.1.9 Interpret clothing and pattern sizes and use height and weight tables.	SB: 88, 89, 90, 91, 101 WB: 77, 78, 79, 81, 84
2.11.03 Calculate the cost of clothing items, including tax.	SB: 88, 89, 91, 95, 99, 101 WB: 77, 78, 79, 84	33. Identify basic clothing.	SB: 88, 89, 91, 99, 101 WB: 77, 78, 84	1.2.1 Interpret advertisements, labels, charts, and price tags in selecting goods and services.	SB: 92, 93, 94, 95, 96, 98, 99, 100, 101 WB: 80, 83, 84, 85, 88, 89
2.11.04 Choose appropriate American clothing sizes for self and family members.	SB: 88, 90, 91, 101 WB: 77, 78, 79, 81, 84	34. Describe clothing colors and sizes.	SB: 88, 89, 90, 91, 101 WB: 77, 78, 79, 81, 84	1.3.7 Interpret information or directions to locate merchandise. 1.3.9 Identify common articles of clothing.	SB: 90, 91, 101 WB: 79, 81, 84
2.15.01 Use colors and shapes to describe objects.	SB: 88, 90, 91 WB: 77, 78, 79, 84	2. Use the present continuous/ progressive tense in communication about events taking place at the moment (e.g., *She's writing.*)	SB: 86, 87 WB: 76	0.1.2 Identify or use appropriate language for informational purposes (e.g., to identify, describe, ask for information, state needs, command, agree or disagree, ask permission).	SB: 86, 87 WB: 76, 78, 80, 81, 85
2.16.04 Use demonstratives.	SB: 94 WB: 79, 82, 84	10. Use determiners appropriately. b. demonstratives: *this, that, these, those*	SB: 95, 97 WB: 80, 81	1.2.1 Interpret advertisements, labels, charts, and price tags in selecting goods and services. 1.6.4 Check sales receipts.	SB: 92, 93, 94, 95 WB: 83, 84, 85
2.16.02 Use regular and irregular verbs (affirmative, negative, yes/no questions, short answers, "wh" questions): – present continuous – *to be* (present) – simple present – simple past – simple future	SB: 86, 87, 101 WB: 76				

Unit 7 DAILY ROUTINES

LCPs	EE Book 1	LAUSD	EE Book 1	CASAS	EE Book 1
2.02.04 Interpret a work schedule (time clock, time sheets, clock-in, sign in).	SB: 106, 111, 114, 116 WB: 98, 100, 102, 103	12. Identify common activities in the classroom, at home and for recreation. 13. Ask and answer questions about common activities.	SB: 102, 103, 105, 107, 111, 114, 116 WB: 90, 91, 92, 93, 102	0.2.4 Converse about daily and leisure activities and personal interests.	SB: 102, 103, 105, 107, 111, 114, 116 WB: 90, 91, 92, 93, 102
2.07.08 Identify practices that promote personal cleanliness and hygiene.	SB: 102, 103, 104, 105 WB: 90, 91, 92, 93	15. Demonstrate understanding and use of simple adverbs. d. of frequency: *always, usually,* etc.	SB: 104, 117 WB: 91, 92, 93, 95, 96	0.2.1 Respond appropriately to common personal information questions.	SB: 108, 109 WB: 92, 93, 94, 95, 96, 97, 98
3.09.01 Identify transportation options. 3.09.02 Identify transportation costs, schedules and practices (exact change, tips).	SB: 90, 91, 92, 94 WB: 94, 97, 98	26. Identify and state day, date and month on a basic calendar.	SB: 104, 109, 112 WB: 91, 100, 101, 103	0.2.4 Converse about daily and leisure activities and personal interests.	SB: 108, 109, 111, 117 WB: 94, 96
2.16.05 Use information questions (*who, what, when, where, how*). 3.16.02 Use common verbs (affirmative, negative, yes/no questions, short answers, "wh" questions): – *to be* – present continuous – simple present tense – future *will*, "going to" – simple past – modals (present)	SB: 107, 108, 109, 111, 117 WB: 94, 96	1. Use simple present tense with: a. the verb *be* in communication about personal information, occupations, feelings, location, names, and descriptions of objects and people, time, and the weather c. the first, second, and third person verb forms of the common verbs used for regularly occurring events (e.g., *I work on Mondays.*)	SB: 103, 108, 110, 117 WB: 91, 93	4.2.1 Interpret wages, wage deductions, benefits, and timekeeping forms. 4.4.3 Interpret job-related signs, charts, diagrams, forms, and procedures, and record information on forms, charts, checklists, etc.	SB: 112, 113 WB: 91, 99, 100, 101
2.16.02 Use regular and irregular verbs (affirmative, negative, yes/no questions, short answers, "wh" questions): – present continuous – *to be* (present) – simple present – simple past – simple future	SB: 102, 103, 105, 107, 110 WB: 90, 92, 93, 95, 98			2.3.1 Interpret clock time. 2.3.2 Identify the months of the year and the days of the week.	SB: 102, 103, 104, 106, 107, 110, 111, 112, 113 WB: 91, 100, 101, 103
2.16.03 Use adverbs. 3.16.08 Use adverbs of time (*yesterday, today,* and *tomorrow*) and adverbs of frequency (*always, sometimes,* and *never*).	SB: 104, 117 WB: 91, 92, 93, 95, 96				
2.08.02 Recognize culturally appropriate concepts of time for school, work, and social activities. 3.08.03 Demonstrate use of a calendar by identifying days of the week and months of the year along with the ability to write date in numerical form.	SB: 104, 109, 112 WB: 91, 100, 101, 103				

Unit 8 LET'S EAT!

LCPs	EE Book 1	LAUSD	EE Book 1	CASAS	EE Book 1

2.07.09 Identify foods and food groups.
 	
3.07.05 Identify basic foods and food groups, recognize nutritional information on food labels, and understand the order of ingredients.
	SB: 118, 119, 121, 122, 133
	
	WB: 104, 106, 107, 109, 114, 116
		16. Use the following question types:
		  c. Wh- questions and answers:
		    i. what, how, where, who
		    ii. how much, how many
		    iii. why, when, which
			SB: 124, 125, 133
			WB: 107, 108, 117
				0.1.2 Identify or use appropriate language for informational purposes (e.g., to identify, describe, ask for information, state needs, command, agree or disagree, ask permission).	SB: 120, 123, 124, 125, 128, 133
					
					WB: 106, 113, 116

2.07.11 Order from a menu.	SB: 128, 129 WB: 114	36. Interpret a simple food label, including basic abbreviations (price per lb., net wt.).	SB: 128, 129 WB: 106, 108, 109, 110, 112	1.2.1 Interpret advertisements, labels, charts, and price tags in selecting goods and services.	SB: 120, 121, 122, 123 WB: 106, 108, 110, 112
2.11.02 Use U.S. units of measure.	SB: 120, 127, 132, 133 WB: 105, 109, 111, 112, 113, 116	1. Use simple present tense with: b. the first, second, and third person verb forms of the verbs *want, need, like,* and *have* in communication about personal wants, needs, likes, dislikes, and possession.	SB: 119, 123, 126, 127, 129 WB: 109	2.7.2 Interpret information about ethnic groups, cultural groups, and language groups. 2.7.3 Interpret information about social issues.	SB: 130, 131, WB: 104
3.16.07 Use information questions.	SB: 120, 123, 124, 125, 128, 133 WB: 106, 113, 116	8. Use the contracted form of *would like* in polite requests (e.g., *I'd like a hamburger*).	SB: 123, 127, 129 WB: 107	1.1.1 Interpret recipes.	SB: 127 WB: 109, 111, 112
2.16.06 Use common and proper nouns.	SB: 118, 123, 127, 133 WB: 104, 105, 106, 108, 109, 110	9. Use nouns appropriately. d. simple countable nouns and uncountable nouns (e.g., *book/books, pencil/pencils, coffee, sugar*)	SB: 118, 119, 127, 133 WB: 105, 106, 108, 109, 110, 111, 112	1.2.2 Compare price or quality to determine the best buys for goods and services.	SB: 120, 121, 123, WB: 106, 111, 112, 114
		35. Identify common foods.	SB: 119, 121, 122, 133 WB: 104, 106, 107, 110, 114, 116		
		17. Use *do/does* in questions in the simple present tense.	SB: 124, 125, 133 WB: 107, 108, 111	1.3.8 Identify common food items.	SB: 119, 121, 122, 133 WB: 104, 106, 107, 110, 114, 116
		18. Use compound sentences with *and, but* (e.g., *Maria's from Mexico, and I'm from Mexico too.*)	SB: 130, 131 WB: 108, 110, 111, 113		

Unit 9 SKILLS AND WORK

LCPs	EE Book 1	LAUSD	EE Book 1	CASAS	EE Book 1
2.01.02 Follow procedures to apply for a job. 3.01.01 Identify different kinds of jobs using simple help-wanted ads including interpreting common abbreviations.	SB: 144, 147 WB: 124, 126, 127, 130	6. Use *can* to express ability and inability (e.g., *I can lift it. I can't lift it.*)	SB: 134, 135, 137, 139, 149 WB: 118, 119, 120, 121, 124, 125, 128	4.1.8 Identify common occupations and the skills and education required for them.	SB: 136, 137, 149 WB: 118, 119, 121, 122
2.01.03 Complete a job application form. 3.01.03 Demonstrate the ability to fill out a job application, write a resume, and include letters of reference.	SB: 146, 147 WB: 126, 127, 131	54. Respond to personal information questions in a simple job interview.	SB: 144, 146, 147 WB: 126, 127	4.1.6 Interpret general work-related vocabulary (e.g., *experience, swing shift*).	SB: 138, 139, 144 WB: 124, 126
2.01.04 Respond to interview questions. 3.01.02 Describe personal work experience and skills. 3.01.06 Demonstrate ability to respond to basic interview questions and recognize acceptable standards of behavior during a job interview.	SB: 136, 139, 145, 146, 147 WB: 121, 126, 127	4. Demonstrate understanding and use of the simple past tense with: b. common regular verbs in communication about completed events or actions c. common irregular verbs in communication about completed events or actions	SB: 142, 143 WB: 122, 123, 129	4.6.4 Report progress on activities, status of assigned tasks, and problems and other situations affecting job completion. 4.6.5 Select and analyze work-related information for a given purpose and communicate it to others orally or in writing.	SB: 145, 149 WB: 118, 119, 120
2.01.07 Interpret simple employment announcements. 3.01.01 Identify different kinds of jobs using simple help-wanted ads including interpreting common abbreviations.	SB: 138, 139, 144 WB: 124, 126	50. Identify common occupations. 51. Identify basic duties of common occupations.	SB: 136, 137, 149 WB: 118, 119, 121, 122	4.2.1 Interpret wages, wage deductions, benefits, and timekeeping forms.	SB: 142, 143 WB: 124
2.02.02 Ask for assistance and clarification on the job. 3.02.03 Demonstrate appropriate treatment of co-workers (politeness and respect). 3.03.02 Demonstrate interpersonal communication skills and positive attitude at work.	SB: 140, 145, 148 WB: 125, 130	52. Read a simple "help wanted" sign or advertisement. 53. Respond to a simple "help wanted" ad or sign in person (e.g., *I saw your sign. Is the job still open?*).	SB: 138, 139, 144 WB: 124, 126	4.1.2 Follow procedures for applying for a job, including interpreting and completing job applications, résumés, and letters of application.	SB: 144, 147 WB: 124, 126, 127, 130
2.04.01 Describe the use of common equipment for home and work. 3.04.01 Demonstrate knowledge of operating equipment necessary for home and work.	SB: 145, 149 WB: 118, 119, 120	4. Demonstrate understanding and use of the simple past tense with: a. the verb *be* in communication about past locations, feelings, occupations, time references, weather (eg., *I was sick yesterday. Yesterday was…*)	SB: 140, 141 WB: 122, 123, 129	4.1.3 Identify and use sources of information about job opportunities such as job descriptions, job ads, and announcements, and about the workforce and job market. 4.1.5 Identify procedures involved in interviewing for a job, such as arranging for an interview, acting and dressing appropriately, and selecting appropriate questions and responses.	SB: 144, 147 WB: 124, 126, 127, 130
2.16.02 Use regular and irregular verbs (affirmative, negative, yes/no questions, short answers, "wh" questions): – present continuous – *to be* (present) – simple present – simple past – simple future	SB: 140, 141, 142, 143, 149 WB: 119, 120, 124, 128				

Unit 10 TAKING A TRIP

LCPs	EE Book 1	LAUSD	EE Book 1	CASAS	EE Book 1
2.13.02 Respond appropriately to weather emergencies. 3.13.01 Describe various weather conditions and respond appropriately to weather emergencies.	SB: 162, 163, 164 WB: 142, 143	57. Call to explain absence or tardiness.	SB: 154, 155 WB: 135	2.2.3 Identify or use different types of transportation in the community, and interpret traffic information.	SB: 150, 154, 165 WB: 132, 134, 138, 140, 144
2.15.05 Fill out various forms.	SB: 160 WB: 135, 143	12. Use adjectives appropriately. a. *be* + adjective (e.g., *She's happy.*) b. adjective + noun (e.g., *He's wearing a red shirt.*)	SB: 158, 159 WB: 136, 144	0.1.2 Identify or use appropriate language for informational purposes (e.g., to identify, describe, ask for information, state needs, command, agree or disagree, ask permission).	SB: 152, 153 WB: 133, 134, 136, 138, 139, 142
2.15.06 Write sentences on a familiar topic using appropriate punctuation.	SB: 159, 161, 162, 163, 165 WB: 133, 136	13. Use non-referential subjects in statements and questions. a. It (*It's/It was*) for time and weather (e.g., *It's 4:00. It's cold.*)	SB: 152, 153, 156, 162, 165 WB: 137, 142	2.1.7 Take and interpret telephone messages, leave messages on answering machines, and interpret recorded messages. 4.6.4 Report progress on activities, status of assigned tasks, and problems and other situations affecting job completion.	SB: 154, 155, WB: 135
2.16.07 Use descriptive adjectives. 3.16.03 Use adjectives: – descriptive – possessive – demonstrative	SB: 153, 155 WB: 133, 136, 144	24. Identify forms of transportation. a. Interpret destination signs on buses, trains, etc. (e.g., *#25 Convention Center*). b. Ask and answer questions about bus routes.	SB: 150, 154, 165 WB: 132, 134, 138, 140, 144	0.1.3 Identify or use appropriate language to influence or persuade (e.g., to caution, request, advise, persuade, negotiate). 0.2.4 Converse about daily and leisure activities and personal interests.	SB: 153, 156, 157, 159, 160 WB: 132, 133, 134, 136, 141, 142
		4. Demonstrate understanding and use of the simple past tense with: a. the verb *be* in communication about past locations, feelings, occupations, time references, weather (e.g., *I was sick yesterday. Yesterday was…*) b. common regular verbs in communication about completed events or actions c. common irregular verbs in communication about completed events or actions	SB: 150, 151, 152, 157, 165 WB: 132, 133, 134, 138, 144	2.2.4 Interpret transportation schedules and fares.	SB: 154, 155, 159 WB: 135, 137, 138, 140, 145
				0.2.1 Respond appropriately to common personal information questions. 1.2.1 Interpret advertisements, labels, charts, and price tags in selecting goods and services.	SB: 151, 157, 158, 160, 161 WB: 134, 135, 137, 138, 139, 142
				2.3.3 Interpret information about weather conditions.	SB: 162, 163, 164 WB: 142, 143

Unit 11 HEALTH MATTERS

LCPs	EE Book 1	LAUSD	EE Book 1	CASAS	EE Book 1
2.06.05 Follow emergency procedure to use 911. 2.10.02 Respond to emergency situations for fire, crime, and medical crises.	SB: 172, 173, 174 WB: 150	21. Call 911 for emergency assistance.	SB: 172, 173, 174 WB: 150	3.1.1 Describe symptoms of illness, including identifying parts of the body; interpret doctor's directions.	SB: 166, 167, 168, 169, 174, 181 WB: 146, 147, 148, 149, 154, 159
3.07.01 Identify body parts.	SB: 168, 169 WB: 147, 154, 159	27. Interpret a simple appointment card with date and time.	SB: 176, 177 WB: 152, 153	2.1.2 Identify emergency numbers and place emergency calls.	SB: 172, 173, 174 WB: 150, 155
2.07.01 Recognize vocabulary related to illnesses and accidents. 3.07.03 Request doctor's appointment, communicate symptoms and injuries, and follow doctor's instructions.	SB: 166, 167, 180, 181 WB: 146, 148, 149, 154, 158	43. Identify major parts of the body.	SB: 168, 169 WB: 147, 154, 159	3.1.3 Identify and utilize appropriate health care services and facilities, including interacting with providers.	SB: 171, 172, 173, 174, 175, 176, 177, 178 WB: 151, 152, 155, 156
2.07.03 Use appropriate health care vocabulary. 3.07.03 Request doctor's appointment, communicate symptoms and injuries, and follow doctor's instructions.	SB: 174, 175, 176, 178 WB: 151, 152, 154, 156	44. Ask about and describe common ailments/symptoms.	SB: 166, 167, 181 WB: 146, 148, 149, 154, 158	0.1.2 Identify or use appropriate language for informational purposes (e.g., to identify, describe, ask for information, state needs, command, agree or disagree, ask permission).	SB: 174, 175, 176, 178 WB: 151, 152, 155, 156
2.07.04 Identify information needed to schedule a doctor's appointment. 3.07.03 Request doctor's appointment, communicate symptoms and injuries, and follow doctor's instructions.	SB: 176, 177 WB: 152, 153	45. Request appropriate over-the-counter medications for simple ailments.	SB: 174, 175 WB: 150, 155	2.1.8 Use the telephone to make and receive routine personal and business calls. 3.1.2 Identify information necessary to make or keep medical and dental appointments.	SB: 170, 171, 176, 177, 180 WB: 152, 153
2.07.06 Use necessary medications in proper dosage. 3.07.04 Read and interpret information on medicine labels.	SB: 175, 177 WB: 151, 155	46. Follow simple instructions during a medical or dental exam.	SB: 172, 173, 177, 181 WB: 151, 155	3.3.3 Identify the difference between prescription, over-the-counter, and generic medications.	SB: 172, 174, 175 WB: 150, 155
2.06.02 Take written telephone messages. 3.07.03 Request doctor's appointment, communicate symptoms and injuries, and follow doctor's instructions.	SB: 170, 171, 180 WB: 152, 153			3.5.1 Interpret nutritional and related information listed on food labels. 3.5.2 Select a balanced diet. 3.5.9 Identify practices that promote physical well being.	SB: 178, 179, WB: 110, 111, 112, 113

Unit 12 PLANING AHEAD

LCPs	EE Book 1	LAUSD	EE Book 1	CASAS	EE Book 1
2.11.06 Compare types of housing. 3.11.04 Identify types of housing (apartment, house, mobile home, condominium) and decipher a lease rental agreement.	SB: 182, 192 WB: 165	38. Identify rooms of a house, furniture and appliances.	SB: 188, 189, 190, 191 WB: 164, 166, 168, 169	0.1.2 Identify or use appropriate language for informational purposes (e.g., to identify, describe, ask for information, state needs, command, agree or disagree, ask permission).	SB: 182, 183, WB: 161, 162, 163, 165, 166, 167, 168, 169
2.11.07 Request service from utility companies. 3.11.05 Identify basic utility companies (water, gas, electric, telephone, and cable).	SB: 188, 190 WB: 166, 167, 173	39. Inquire about apartment and house rentals.	SB: 192, 193 WB: 165, 173	0.1.6 Clarify or request clarification. 7.1.4 Establish, maintain, and utilize a physical system of organization, such as notebooks, files, calendars, folders, and checklists.	SB: 184, 185, 186, 187 WB: 165, 166, 167
2.04.01 Describe the use of common equipment for home and work.	SB: 188, 189 WB: 164, 166, 168, 169	3. Use be + going to to indicate future (e.g., I'm going to go to work tomorrow.)	SB: 182, 183, 186, 189, 197 WB: 160, 161, 162, 163, 164, 172	7.2.7 Identify factors involved in making decisions, including considering goals, constraints, and consequences, and weighing alternatives.	SB: 186, 187 WB: 160, 161, 167, 170, 171
3.11.03 Read sales ads and compare prices (clothing, cars, and food).	SB: 182, 183 WB: 166, 172	11. Use personal pronouns appropriately. b. object pronouns: me, you, her, him, it, us, them	SB: 184, 185 WB: 160, 161, 166, 172, 173	1.4.1 Identify different kinds of housing, areas of the home, and common household items. 1.5.2 Plan for major purchases.	SB: 188, 189, 191 WB: 164, 165, 166, 168

3.16.02 Use common verbs (affirmative, negative, yes/no questions, short answers, "wh" questions):
  – to be
  – present continuous
  – simple present tense
  – future will, "going to"
  – simple past
  – modals (present)
				1.4.2 Select appropriate housing by interpreting classified ads, signs, and other information.	SB: 190, 191, 192, 197
					WB: 165

				7.4.3 Identify, utilize, or create devices or processes for remembering information.	SB: 190, 191 WB: 164, 165, 166, 170
				7.1.2 Demonstrate an organized approach to achieving goals, including identifying and prioritizing tasks and setting and following an effective schedule. 7.1.4 Establish, maintain, and utilize a physical system of organization, such as notebooks, files, calendars, folders, and checklists.	SB: 194, 195, 196 WB: 163, 164, 165, 166, 170

Letters and Numbers

1 LISTEN AND CIRCLE. Listen to the letters. Circle the ones you hear.

1. D G Ⓒ
2. A F N
3. M L H
4. K I L
5. T S P

6. O A E
7. R U Z
8. Y J W
9. C S Z
10. U A I

2 LISTEN AND WRITE the letters you hear.

1. _H_ _I_
2. _____ _____
3. _____ _____
4. _____ _____
5. _____ _____

6. _____ _____
7. _____ _____
8. _____ _____
9. _____ _____ _____
10. _____ _____ _____

3 LISTEN AND CIRCLE. Listen to the people spell their names. Circle the names.

1. Sandra (Brenda)
2. Maria Tiara
3. Luis Lee
4. Victor Peter
5. Patty Betty

6. Kevin Kendra
7. Sam Stan
8. Tim Tom
9. Susan Susanne
10. Greg Craig

4 LISTEN AND WRITE the missing letters.

1. D _A_ VI _D_
2. A ___ N ___
3. J ___ ___ IA
4. ___ E ___ TO ___
5. S ___ ___ IA

6. RA ___ ___
7. H ___ ___ O
8. ___ O ___ A ___
9. ___ I ___ ___ ___
10. E ___ ___ ___ T

5 **LISTEN** to the numbers. Circle the numbers you hear.
WCD, 6

1. 5   8   ③   **8.** 20   70   50

2. 4   9   2   **9.** 40   30   80

3. 1   6   7   **10.** 90   60   70

4. 12   15   19   **11.** 10   15   11

5. 11   17   18   **12.** 80   18   8

6. 14   10   13   **13.** 15   50   60

7. 18   16   14   **14.** 3   13   30

6 **LISTEN** to the numbers. Write the missing numbers.

WCD, 7

1. 4 __2__ 39   **8.** 1 _____ 5 _____

2. 94 _____   **9.** _____ 20 _____

3. 2 _____ 5 _____   **10.** 2 _____ 0 _____

4. 8 _____ 4 _____   **11.** 7 _____ 23 _____

5. _____ 2 _____ 6   **12.** _____ 60 _____ 8

6. _____ 10 _____   **13.** 45 _____ _____ _____

7. _____ 52 _____   **14.** 9 _____ 2 _____ _____

7 **LISTEN** to the numbers. Circle the numbers you hear.

WCD, 8

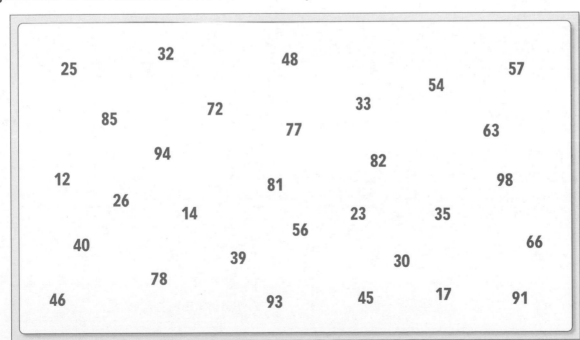

Classroom Directions

1 **CIRCLE** the correct words.

1
- **a.** Open your book.
- **b.** Raise your hand.

2
- **a.** Listen.
- **b.** Read.

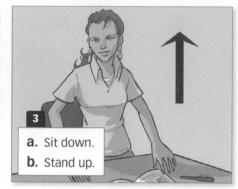

3
- **a.** Sit down.
- **b.** Stand up.

4
- **a.** Turn to page 15.
- **b.** Open your book.

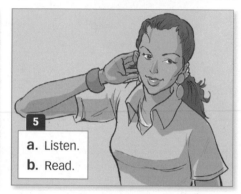

5
- **a.** Listen.
- **b.** Read.

6
- **a.** Take out your pen.
- **b.** Raise your hand.

7
- **a.** Open your book.
- **b.** Write your name.

8
- **a.** Listen.
- **b.** Raise your hand.

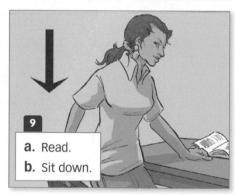

9
- **a.** Read.
- **b.** Sit down.

2 **WRITE.** Complete the sentences. Use the words in the box.

name	book	page	~~up~~	down	hand	pen

1. Stand _____*up*_____ .

2. Sit _____ .

3. Take out a _____ .

4. Write your _____ .

5. Open your _____ .

6. Turn to _____ 15.

7. Raise your _____ .

Grammar: Parts of Speech

1 **WRITE** the letter under the picture.

| 1 | 2 | 3 | 4 | 5 | 6 |

a. a school   **d.** read

b. tall   **e.** a teacher

c. a book   **f.** talk

2 **WRITE** the words in the chart.

a book	talk	study	tall	happy
a school	a pen	red	write	

Nouns	Verbs	Adjectives
a book		

3 **LISTEN.** Circle the correct words.

1. I / (We) study English.

2. **He / It** is tall.

3. **We / They** walk to school.

4. **You / We** read books.

5. **It / She** is happy.

6. **We / You** listen to the teacher.

7. **We / I** write my name.

8. **You / We** talk at school.

9. **I / They** sit down.

10. **You / We** stand up.

Lesson 1

1 **MATCH** the personal information words with the examples. Write the letters.

___e___ **1.** city   **a.** Diana

_____ **2.** telephone number   **b.** 33607

_____ **3.** first name   **c.** 1543 Central Street, Tampa

_____ **4.** zip code   **d.** montego123@people.net

_____ **5.** address   **e.** Tampa

_____ **6.** last name   **f.** married

_____ **7.** email address   **g.** (813) 555-4785

_____ **8.** marital status   **h.** Montego

2 **WHAT ABOUT YOU?** Complete the form about you.

Last name: _____   First name: _____

Address: _____

City: _____   State: _____

Zip Code: _____   Telephone Number: _____

Email: _____

Marital Status: ☐ single   ☐ married

3 **WRITE.** Complete the sentences. Use *am*, *is*, or *are*.

1. My name ___is___ Paul.

2. I _____ a student.

3. Ms. Nelson _____ my teacher.

4. Ana and I _____ from Canada.

5. We _____ married.

6. David and Marcos _____ students.

7. They _____ from Honduras.

8. My telephone number _____ (408) 555-1357.

Lesson 2

1 WRITE. Complete the paragraph. Use *am not*, *is not*, or *are not*.

I'm Stefan Marat. I (1) ____am not____ Teresa.

My last name (2) _____ Mendoza. I'm

married. I (3) _____ single. My address is

512 Western Avenue, San Jose. It (4) _____

512 Maple Street. Elena and I are from Russia. We

(5) _____ from Mexico. The letters are from

Mexico. They (6) _____ my letters.

2 WRITE. Unscramble the words. Then write them in the form.

1. r / e / a / s / d / d / s ____address____

2. t / s / i / r / f m / a / e / n _____

3. t / i / y / c _____

4. g / i / n / l / e / s _____

5. n / p / l / e / t / e / o / e / h m / b / n / u / e / r _____

6. p / z / i d / e / o / c _____

Last name: _Marat_____   _____: _Stefan____

_____: _512 Western Avenue_____

_____: _San Jose_____   State: _California_

_____: _95129_____   _____: _813-555-3597_

Email: _____

Marital Status: ☐ _____   ☐ married

Lesson 3

WCD, 10

1 **LISTEN** and circle the number you hear.

1. 15   (50)

2. 19   90

3. 13   30

4. 16 Main Street   60 Main Street

5. 18 Center Road   80 Center Road

6. 1820 Park Street   8020 Park Street

7. 555-1217   555-1270

8. 555-1490   555-4019

WCD, 11

2 **LISTEN** and write the number you hear.

1. My address is _____117_____ Bayview Street.

2. Stefan's address is _____ Lowell Avenue.

3. The address is _____ Woods Avenue.

4. The telephone number is 555-_____.

5. Please call 555-_____.

6. Maria's phone number is 555-_____.

3 **WRITE.** Complete the conversation. Use the words in the box.

It's nice	from	~~my name's~~	Hi	I'm	to meet you	student

Lin: Hi, (1) ____*my name's*____ Lin. (2) _____ from Korea.

Carina: (3) _____, Lin. My name's Carina. I'm (4) _____ Mexico.

          I'm a (5) _____.

Lin: I'm a student, too.

Carina: It's nice (6) _____.

Lin: (7) _____ to meet you, too.

Culture and Communication — *Greetings*

1 **LOOK** and read.

1
Mother: Good morning, Tom.
Tom: Hi, Mom.

2
Mr. Santos: Good afternoon. I'm Mr. Santos.
Kathy: Hello, Mr. Santos. I'm Kathy Green. Pleased to meet you.

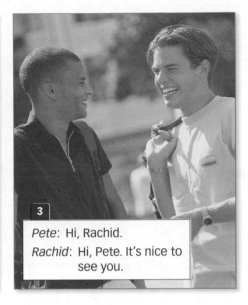

3
Pete: Hi, Rachid.
Rachid: Hi, Pete. It's nice to see you.

2 **LISTEN** and read. Then practice with a partner.

WCD, 12

Cecelia:	Good morning, Mr. Nelson.
Mr. Nelson:	Hello, Cecelia. It's nice to see you.
Cecelia:	How are you doing today?
Mr. Nelson:	I'm OK, and you?
Cecelia:	I'm fine, thanks. Well, I've got to run. <u>Take care</u>.
Mr. Nelson:	OK. See you later.

Useful Expressions

To end a conversation
Good-bye.
See you later.
Talk to you later.
Take care.

3 **WHAT ABOUT YOU?** Complete the conversation.

You:	_____, Mr. Nelson.
Mr. Nelson:	Hello. It's nice to see you.
You:	How are you doing today?
Mr. Nelson:	I'm OK, and you?
You:	I'm fine, thanks. Well, _____.
Mr. Nelson:	OK. _____.

Lesson 4

1 **WRITE** the occupation. Use *a* or *an*.

| housekeeper | salesclerk | nurse | construction worker | police officer | office assistant |

1 She's _____a salesclerk_____.

2 He's _____.

3 He's _____.

4 He's _____.

5 He's _____.

6 She's _____.

2 **WRITE.** Complete the sentences. Use the singular or plural of the noun.

1. (server) Mei is _____a server_____.

2. (cook) Tomas and I are _____.

3. (doctor) Daniela is _____.

4. (actor) Sam and Bill are _____.

5. (teacher) Julio is _____.

6. (firefighter) You and Ana are _____.

7. (student) We are _____.

8. (housekeeper) I am _____.

3 **CIRCLE** the correct word.

1. Two **child / children** are students.

2. One **child / children** is not a student.

3. Three **man / men** are firefighters.

4. One **man / men** is not a teacher.

5. One **woman / women** is from China.

6. Four **woman / women** are from Canada.

7. Two **person / people** are married.

8. One **person / people** is single.

Lesson 5

1 **LOOK AND WRITE.** Look at the chart. Then circle the correct word to complete the sentences.

				Sonia's Class				
Name	Sonia	Eric	Hassa	David	Irina	Ahmed	Ana	Alan
Male		✓		✓		✓		✓
Female	✓		✓		✓		✓	
Single	✓	✓			✓	✓		✓
Married			✓	✓			✓	
Occupation	nurse	taxi driver	server	nurse	housekeeper	taxi driver	server	teacher

Hi. My name is Sonia Muñoz. I am from Honduras. I am also a (1) **housekeeper / nurses / student** Eight (2) **student / people / married people** are in my class. Alan is a (3) **teacher / man / server**. One (4) **nurse / women / woman** (Irina) is a housekeeper. Two men are (5) **taxi drivers / taxi driver / student**. David and I are (6) **men / nurse / nurses**. Two (7) **woman / women / person** (Hassa and Ana) are servers. Three (8) **student / servers / people** (Hassa, David, and Ana) are married. What about you?

2 **WRITE** the words.

1. 1 student + 1 student = 2 __s__ __t__ __u__ __d__ __e__ __n__ | t | __s__

2. 1 man + 1 man = 2 ____ | | ____

3. 4 women – 3 women = 1 ____ ____ ____ | | ____

4. 1 child + 1 child = 2 | | ____ ____ ____ ____ ____ ____

5. 10 children – 9 children = 1 ____ | | ____ ____

6. 1 person + 1 person = 2 ____ ____ ____ ____ | | ____

7. 5 people – 4 people = 1 ____ ____ | | ____ ____

3 **LOOK** at the letters in the boxes in Activity 5. Write the letters to find an occupation.

__t__ ____ ____ ____ ____ ____ ____

Family Connection — *Activities at the Library*

1 **READ** and look.

2 **LOOK** and circle *children*, *students*, *men*, and *women*.

County Library
Featured Events and Classes
Fall 2009

Crafts for Children
Make things at the library.

Homework Helpers
Volunteers give students help with homework.

Storytime
Children listen to stories.

Talk Time
Men and women practice speaking English.

Citizenship Class
Learn how to become a citizen.

Crafts for Adults
Men and women can make things, too.

Book Discussion for Women
Women read and talk about books.

Films and Discussion
Watch films and talk about them with other people.

3 CIRCLE *yes* or *no*.

1. Four classes are for children.   yes   (no)

2. Storytime is for children.   yes   no

3. Two classes are for crafts.   yes   no

4. Book Discussion is for men and women.   yes   no

5. Talk Time is not for children.   yes   no

6. Citizenship Class is for children.   yes   no

7. Homework Helpers is for students.   yes   no

8. Films and Discussion is not for men and women.   yes   no

4 REAL-LIFE LESSON. Write the names of classes in the chart below.

In your school or library, what classes are for children, men, and women?

Classes for . . .	Class Name	Class Description
Children		
Women		
Men		
Mixed Groups	*Baby Sing*	*Moms and babies learn songs together.*

Community Connection — *Write a Letter*

1 **READ** the conversation.

> *Fatah:* Hi, I'm Fatah. Do you live here, too?
>
> *Tanya:* Yes, I do. My name's Tanya. Nice to meet you, Fatah. Where are you from?
>
> *Fatah:* I'm from Egypt. What about you?
>
> *Tanya:* I'm from Russia. I'm a nurse, but here I'm a housekeeper.
>
> *Fatah:* I see. I'm a teacher in Egypt, but here I'm a student. I'm in a class at the Community School.
>
> *Tanya:* Me, too. Mr. Carlson's my teacher. Is he your teacher?
>
> *Fatah:* No, my teacher is Mrs. Beda.
>
> *Tanya:* Well, maybe I'll see you later.
>
> *Fatah:* OK. Bye.

2 **CIRCLE** *yes* or *no*.

1. Fatah is from Egypt.   (yes)   no
2. Tanya and Fatah are nurses.   yes   no
3. Fatah is a teacher in Egypt.   yes   no
4. Fatah is not a student at the Community School.   yes   no
5. Mr. Carlson is a teacher at the Community School.   yes   no
6. Mrs. Beda is a student in the class.   yes   no

3 **WRITE** answers to the questions.

1. What's your name? _____

2. Where are you from? _____

3. What's your occupation in your country? _____

4. What's your occupation now? _____

5. What's the name of your school? _____

6. What's the name of your teacher? _____

4 **WRITE** a letter to your teacher or a friend about yourself. Use the answers from Activity 3.

Dear _____,

    My name is _____

_____

_____

_____

_____

_____

_____

_____

_____

                                        Sincerely,

                              _____

5 **REAL-LIFE LESSON.** Ask a person (a neighbor or a person at work) the questions. Write their answers in the chart. Write one question from you.

Question	Answer
1. What's your name?	
2. Where are you from?	
3. What's your occupation in your country?	
4. What's your occupation now?	
5. Are you a student?	
6. What's the name of your school?	
7. What's the name of your teacher?	
8. _____	

Career Connection — *Make Copies*

1 **READ** the instructions for the machine.

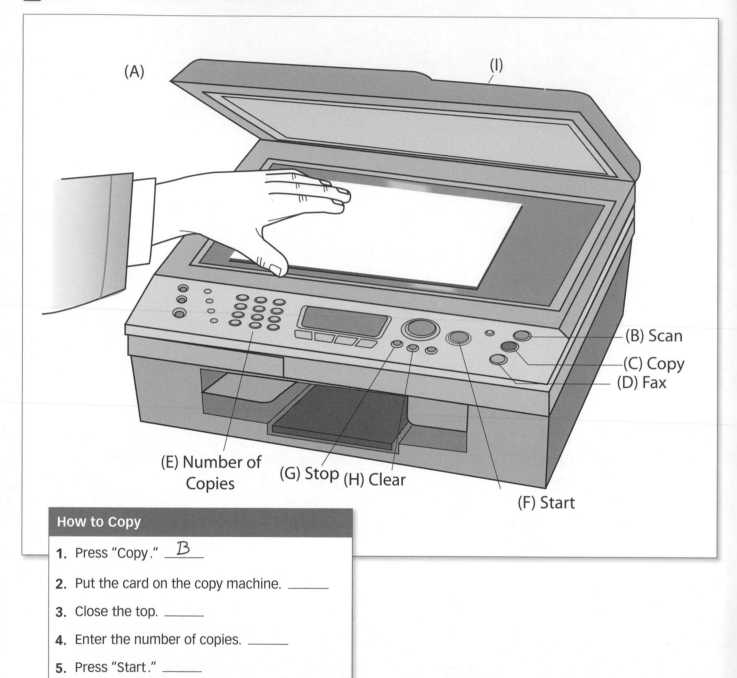

(A)

(I)

(B) Scan

(C) Copy

(D) Fax

(E) Number of Copies

(G) Stop (H) Clear

(F) Start

How to Copy

1. Press "Copy." ___B___

2. Put the card on the copy machine. _____

3. Close the top. _____

4. Enter the number of copies. _____

5. Press "Start." _____

6. Take the copy and the card.

2 **WRITE** the letter of the part or button Isabel uses on the machine.

3 **READ** the sentences. Cross out the word that is wrong. Then write the correct word.

1. Press ~~"Scan."~~ _____ Copy _____

2. Put the card on the computer. _____

3. Open the top. _____

4. Enter the telephone number. _____

5. Press "Stop." _____

6. Take the copy machine and the card. _____

🖥 Technology Connection: Email Addresses

A **LOOK** at the email. Circle the email addresses.

myschool.com

| Check mail | Compose | Search mail | Search Web | |

(6) **Inbox**

(1) **Draft**

(1) **Sent**

Bulk

Trash

To: tdaysun@myschool.com
From: bmarcos@myschool.com

Hi Tanya. How are you?
Write back!

Bye for now,
Beto

B **LOOK** at the names and the email addresses. Write the addresses of these other students.

Tanya Daysun:	tdaysun@myschool.com
Beto Marcos:	bmarcos@myschool.com
Helena Chavez:	
Chu Peng:	
Mohan Singh:	
Katarina Klein:	
_____ (your name)	_____ (your email)

Practice Test

LISTENING: Listen to the conversations. Then choose the correct answer for each sentence.

1. What is the man's first name? _____
   A. José
   B. Eva
   C. Colombia
   D. Paez

2.
   A. I'm from the United States.
   B. It's nice to meet you, too.
   C. Hi, I'm Laura Smith.
   D. I'm a student.

3. What's the man's name? _____
   A. Nick Worker
   B. Clark Street
   C. Nick Clark
   D. East Street

4. What is his occupation? _____
   A. construction worker
   B. nurse
   C. taxi driver
   D. firefighter

5. What is his address? _____
   A. 18 Clark Street
   B. 15 Beat Street
   C. 20 Main Street
   D. 50 East Street

GRAMMAR: Choose the correct word to complete each sentence.

6. You _____ from China.
   A. am
   B. is
   C. are
   D. a

7. Mai _____ a student.
   A. am
   B. is
   C. are
   D. a

8. I _____ not a teacher.
   A. am
   B. is
   C. are
   D. an

9. _____ are nurses.
   A. I
   B. He
   C. It
   D. They

10. Alex is _____ actor.
    A. a
    B. an
    C. are
    D. not

11. Paul and Sara are _____ .
    A. a teacher
    B. a nurse
    C. servers
    D. a server

VOCABULARY: Choose the best word to complete the sentence.

12. My _____ is 118 Central Avenue.
    A. city
    B. telephone
    C. zip code
    D. address

13. Pedro is not married. He's _____.
    A. female
    B. a server
    C. single
    D. servers

14. My _____ is 27720.
    A. zip code
    B. email address
    C. telephone number
    D. address

15. My _____ is (707) 555-1780.
    A. zip code
    B. address
    C. telephone number
    D. email address

16. Alex is from _____.
    A. student
    B. Russia
    C. married
    D. teacher

READING: Look at the form. Choose the correct answer.

Last name: _Garvey_   First name: _Lena_

Address: _1650 Southside Road_

City: _Watertown_   State: _MA_

Zip Code: _02144_   Telephone Number: _(617) 555-7032_

Email: _lgarvey@myschool.com_

Marital Status: ☐ single   ☑ married

17. The last name is _____.
    A. Garvey
    B. Lena
    C. Southside
    D. Watertown

18. The city is _____.
    A. Watertown
    B. married
    C. MA
    D. 02144

19. Lena is _____.
    A. single
    B. married
    C. 02144
    D. students

20. The address is _____.
    A. lgarvey@myschool.com
    B. Watertown
    C. (617) 555-7032
    D. 1650 Southside Road

UNIT 2 People

Lesson 1

1 MATCH the questions with the answers. Write the letters.

___c___ **1.** Are you shy?

_____ **2.** Are Dan and Miko funny?

_____ **3.** Is Susie tall?

_____ **4.** Is Alex neat?

_____ **5.** Are you hardworking?

_____ **6.** Are they young?

_____ **7.** Are you and Dan serious?

_____ **8.** Is Hiro thin?

a. No, I'm not. I'm lazy.

b. No, he isn't. He's heavy.

c. No, I'm not. I'm outgoing.

d. No, they aren't. They're old.

e. No, they aren't. They're serious.

f. No, we're not. We're funny.

g. No, he isn't. He's messy.

h. No, she isn't. She's short.

2 WRITE answers to the questions.

1. Are you neat?   Yes, ____I am____ .

2. Is Alex short?   Yes, _____ .

3. Is Ana shy?   No, _____ .

4. Are Ben and Tom tall?   No, _____ .

5. Are you serious?   No, _____ .

6. Is Mr. Peters lazy?   No, _____ .

7. Are the students outgoing? Yes, _____ .

8. Is Linda pretty?   Yes, _____ .

 3 WHAT ABOUT YOU? Answer the questions.

1. Are you lazy?   ____Yes, I am____ . or ____No, I'm not____ .

2. Are you shy?   _____ . or _____ .

3. Are you neat?   _____ . or _____ .

4. Are you serious? _____ . or _____ .

5. Are you tall?   _____ . or _____ .

6. Are you young?   _____ . or _____ .

Lesson 2

1 **LOOK AND WRITE.** Look at the pictures. Write questions using the cues. Then write the answers.

1
(Sally/neat)

Is Sally neat?
No, she isn't. She's messy.

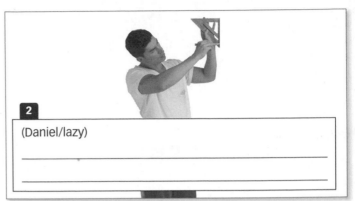

2
(Daniel/lazy)

_____
_____

3
(Sam and Maria/old)

_____
_____

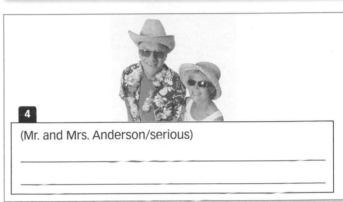

4
(Mr. and Mrs. Anderson/serious)

_____
_____

2 **WRITE.** Complete the paragraph. Use the words in the box.

| funny | ~~young~~ | outgoing | an actor | a cook | heavy | shy | hardworking |

My name is Sam. I'm not old. I'm (1) _____young_____ . I'm not lazy. I'm

(2) _____ and serious. I'm not messy. I'm shy. I'm not (3) _____ .

I'm tall, but I'm not thin. I work in a restaurant. I'm (4) _____ .

I'm Adam. I'm not thin. I'm (5) _____ . I'm outgoing. I'm not

(6) _____ . I'm not old, but I'm not young. I'm not serious. I'm

(7) _____ and hardworking. I work in a theater. I'm (8) _____ .

Lesson 3

1 LOOK. Put the conversation in order.

_____ Oh. Is she the tall and thin one?

_____ OK. Thank you.

___1___ Excuse me. Are you Tanya?

_____ No. That's Carla. Tanya is short and pretty.

_____ No, I'm not. Tanya is over there.

2 CIRCLE the correct answer.

1.	Is Tanya tall?	Yes, she is.	No, she isn't.
2.	Is Carla tall?	Yes, she is.	No, she isn't.
3.	Is Carla thin?	Yes, she is.	No, she isn't.
4.	Is Tanya thin?	Yes, she is.	No, she isn't.
5.	Is Tanya short?	Yes, she is.	No, she isn't.
6.	Is Tanya pretty?	Yes, she is.	No, she isn't.
7.	Is Carla short?	Yes, she is.	No, she isn't.
8.	Is Carla heavy?	Yes, she is.	No, she isn't.
9.	Is she shy?	Yes, she is.	No, she isn't.
10.	Is she young?	Yes, she is.	No, he isn't.

3 LISTEN to the questions. Circle the words you hear.

WCD, 14

1. (Is he)/ Is she from India? _____ *No, he isn't.* _____

2. Is he / Is she a nurse? _____

3. Is he / Is she tall and hardworking? _____

4. Is he / Is she serious? _____

5. Is he / Is she neat? _____

6. Is he / Is she young? _____

7. Is he / Is she pretty? _____

8. Is he / Is she short? _____

LISTEN again. Write the answers in Activity 3.

Culture and Communication — *Describe People*

1 **LISTEN.** Read the conversation.

A: I'm short. I'm not tall.

B: You're not short. You're medium height.

A: I'm too heavy.

B: No, you're not heavy. You're average weight.

A: You're so thin!

B: Well, I'm average weight, too.

A: Are you messy?

B: No, I'm not. I'm not very neat, but I'm hardworking.

A: I'm hardworking, too. And I'm outgoing.

B: I'm not. I'm shy.

A: You're funny!

B: No, I'm serious!

2 **WRITE** the words in order.

1. short

   short, _____*medium height, tall*_____

2. heavy   thin   average weight

   thin, _____

3. neat   not very neat   messy

   messy, _____

4. middle aged   old   young

   young, _____

5. hardworking   lazy   not very lazy

   lazy, _____

6. not very outgoing   shy   outgoing

   shy, _____

Lesson 4

1 **LOOK** at the picture of Tonio's family. Complete the sentences. Use the words in the box.

grandfather	grandmother	sister	brother	husband	wife
son	daughter	children	~~father~~	mother	

1. Tonio is Miguel's _____ *father* _____ .

2. Julia is Miguel's _____ .

3. Lilia is Miguel's _____ .

4. Claire is Miguel's _____ .

5. Tonio is Claire's _____ .

6. Miguel is Julia's _____ .

7. Oscar is Julia's _____ .

8. Julia and Miguel are Tonio and Claire's _____ .

2 **LOOK AND WRITE.** Look at the picture in Activity 1. Complete the sentences with possessive nouns.

1. Miguel is _____ *Claire's or Tonio's* _____ son.

2. Tonio is _____ son.

3. Oscar is _____ father.

4. Lilia is _____ mother.

5. Julia is _____ daughter.

6. Lilia is _____ grandmother.

3 **WRITE.** Complete the sentences. Use *my, your, his, her, our,* or *their*.

1. I have a brother. _____ *His* _____ name is Paul.

2. We have two cousins. _____ cousins' names are Susie and David.

3. Susie is tall and thin. _____ brother is tall, too.

4. Are you married? What's _____ husband's name?

5. They have two sisters. _____ sisters are nurses.

6. I have an uncle. _____ uncle is a construction worker.

7. You and Mauricio have two children. _____ sons are handsome.

Lesson 5

1 **WEIGHT.** In most countries, weight is in grams and kilograms. In the United States, weight is in pounds and ounces.

Complete the sentences. Convert kilograms to pounds.

1 kg = 2.2 lb.	2 kg = 4.4 lb.	3 kg = _____	kg x 2.2 = weight in lb.

1. Binh is 5 years old. His weight is 15 kg, or _____ lb.

   15 x 2.2 = _____

2. Rachid is 8 years old. His weight is 20 kg, or _____ lb.

   20 x 2.2 = _____

3. Seydor is 12 years old. His weight is 60 kg, or _____ lb.

4. Yuri is 9 years old. His weight is 30 kg, or _____ lb.

LOOK at the chart of weights. Circle the answers.

Average weight (boys aged 5–12)			
Age	**Weight in Pounds**	**Age**	**Weight in Pounds**
5	40 lbs.	9	62 lbs.
6	46 lbs.	10	72 lbs.
7	50 lbs.	11	80 lbs.
8	56 lbs.	12	90 lbs.

1. Binh is **thin / average weight / heavy**.

2. Rachid is **thin / average weight / heavy**.

3. Seydor is **thin / average weight / heavy**.

4. Yuri is **thin / average weight / hcavy**.

2 **SHE'S MY COUSIN!** Complete the sentences. Use the words in the box.

brother	aunt	sister	grandfather	~~cousin~~	uncle

1. She's the daughter of my aunt and uncle. She's my _____*cousin*_____.

2. He's the husband of my grandmother. He's my _____.

3. She's the wife of my uncle. She's my _____.

4. He's the son of my mother and father. He's my _____.

5. He's the brother of my father. He's my _____.

6. She's the daughter of my mother and father. She's my _____.

Family Connection — *Emergency Contacts*

1 LOOK at the emergency contact form. Circle the names of people on the form.

East Side Community School					
Name of Student					
Last	Milano	**First**	Kevin	**Gender**	M
Parent / Guardian					
Name	Nancy Milano	**Relationship**	mother		
Address	329 Weston Street				
City	Jacksonville	**State**	FL	**Zip Code**	32211
Telephone #	(904) 555-3298	**Work Phone**	(904) 555-8822		
Emergency Contact					
Emergency #	(904) 555-8822	**Name**	Nancy Milano	**Relationship**	mother
If Unavailable (2ⁿᵈ Emergency Contact)					
2ⁿᵈ Emergency #	(904) 555-4176	**Name**	Nick Milano	**Relationship**	grandfather
Physician					
Name	Dr. Saleem Aziz	**Telephone #**	(904) 555-1768		
Additional Medical Information					
Allergic to penicillin					

2 WRITE. Answer the questions about the form.

1. What is the student's name? _____

2. Who is Nancy Milano? _____

3. What is their phone number? _____

4. What is Nancy's phone number at work? _____

5. Who is Nick Milano? _____

6. What is his phone number? _____

7. In an emergency, the school calls _____.

8. Then the school calls _____.

9. Who is Saleem Aziz? _____

10. What is penicillin? Use a dictionary to find the answer. _____

3 FIND AND MATCH. Find the words on the form. Then match the words with their meanings or symbols.

_____ **1.** parent

_____ **2.** unavailable

_____ **3.** emergency

_____ **4.** contact

_____ **5.** relationship

_____ **6.** physician

a. father, sister, uncle . . .

b. doctor

c. name of a person to call

d. mother or father

e. 🔥 ➕

f. does not answer

4 REAL-LIFE LESSON. Interview a friend or a teacher about emergency situations. Write who the school calls.

Fire in the School

Fire department, police

Parents or emergency contacts

Student Is Hurt or Sick

_____

_____

Student Is Poisoned

_____

_____

Flood

_____

_____

Snow

_____

_____

Emergency

_____

_____

Community Connection — *Emergency Numbers*

1 **MATCH** the symbols with the words.

_____ 1. 🚑   **a.** hospital

_____ 2. 🔥   **b.** poison

_____ 3. ☠   **c.** call

_____ 4. 👮   **d.** ambulance

_____ 5. **H**   **e.** fire

_____ 6. 📞   **f.** police

2 **LOOK** at the list of emergency phone numbers. Circle the words from Activity 1.

Emergency Numbers	
Fire	911
Police	911
Ambulance	911
Poison	555-4321
Doctor Singh	*555-1200*
County Hospital	555-5000
Neighbor *Jana*	555-3827
Mom (work)	*555-2365*
Eva (cell)	*555-0924*

3 **READ** the conversation. Complete the sentences with the words in the box.

wife	truck	fire	~~address~~	emergency

Operator: 911 Operator. What's your _____*address*_____ ?

Bruno: My house is on _____ !

Operator: What's your name and _____ ?

Bruno: My name is Bruno Amado. I live at 4123 East Street in Pasadena.

Operator: Who is with you?

Bruno: My _____ and my daughter.

Operator: OK. Do not go back inside. A fire _____ is on the way.

4 **CIRCLE** the answers. Use the telephone numbers in Activity 2.

1. Call 555-5000 for **a fire / the police / the hospital**.

2. Call 911 for **Mom at work / a fire / the doctor**.

3. Call 555-4321 for **Jana / an ambulance / poison**.

4. Call 911 for **Eva / an ambulance / the hospital**.

5. Call 555-1200 for the **hospital / the doctor / a neighbor**.

6. Call _____ for Eva.

7. Call _____ for a family member.

8. The telephone number for the police is _____.

5 **WRITE.** Complete the paragraph. Use the words in the box. Use a dictionary to help you.

firefighter	hospital	fire truck	EMT	~~doctor~~	ambulance

A _____*doctor*_____ is a person who cares for you when you are sick. This person works in

a _____. A firefighter drives a _____ and puts out fires.

An _____ is an Emergency Medical Technician. This person drives an

_____. When you call 911, a _____ or an EMT comes to

your house.

6 **REAL-LIFE LESSON.** Write your list of emergency phone numbers.

My Emergency Phone List

Fire _____

Police _____

Ambulance _____

Poison _____

Doctor _____ _____

_____ Hospital _____

Neighbor _____ _____

_____ (work) _____

_____ (cell) _____

Career Connection — *Ask for Office Supplies*

1 READ the conversation.

> *Isabel:* Is that young man your husband?
>
> *Mimi:* No, he's the new receptionist.
>
> *Isabel:* Oh. What's he like?
>
> *Mimi:* He's shy and funny.
>
> *Isabel:* Is he a good receptionist?
>
> *Mimi:* Well, he's hardworking, but he's not very neat.
>
> *Isabel:* I see.

2 CIRCLE *yes* or *no*.

1.	The new receptionist is female.	yes	(no)
2.	The new receptionist is young.	yes	no
3.	Mimi is the wife of the new receptionist.	yes	no
4.	The receptionist is not serious.	yes	no
5.	He's hardworking.	yes	no
6.	He's very neat.	yes	no
7.	He's shy.	yes	no
8.	He's not outgoing.	yes	no

3 WRITE words to describe the new receptionist and yourself.

The new receptionist is . . .	I am . . .

Technology Connection: When to Use a Cell Phone

4 **READ** the sentence and circle *Use* or *Don't use*.

1. Use / **Don't use** a cell phone at a movie.

2. Use / **Don't use** a cell phone in a car.

3. Use / **Don't use** a cell phone at work.

4. Use / **Don't use** a cell phone at home.

5. Use / **Don't use** a cell phone in class.

6. Use / **Don't use** a cell phone in a hospital.

7. Use / **Don't use** a cell phone in a restaurant.

5 **READ** the telephone conversation. Then write the message.

A: Good morning, Central Hospital. How may I help you?

B: Hi. Is Dr. Vasquez available?

A: No, I'm sorry. She isn't. She's with a patient. Can I take a message?

B: Sure. This is Hector Garcia. I'm at work, but my cell phone number is 508-555-1742.

A: 508-555-1472?

B: No, it's 1742.

A: Oh, OK. 555-1742.

B: That's right. Please tell her to call me. Thanks.

Important message

To: _____

From: _____

Phone: _____

Message: _____

_____

_____

_____

_____

Tip
Use a cell phone at work only for very important calls. It is polite to go outside or to a quiet place.

Practice Test

LISTENING: Listen to the conversations. Then choose the correct answer for each sentence.

1. Who is a nurse?
   A. a doctor
   B. a hospital
   C. Emma
   D. Dr. Abel

2. Choose the best answer.
   A. No, she isn't. She's hardworking.
   B. Yes, she is. She's tall and heavy.
   C. Yes, she is. She's shy and funny.
   D. No, she isn't. She's tall and heavy.

3. Who is on the phone?
   A. Mary's father
   B. Mary's sister
   C. Mary
   D. Mary's brother

4. What is his name?
   A. Bill
   B. John
   C. Eric
   D. Julie

5. What is his phone number?
   A. 555-3548
   B. 555-5274
   C. 555-1357
   D. 555-5384

GRAMMAR AND VOCABULARY: Choose the correct word to complete each sentence.

6. Is he your son? Yes, _____ .
   A. I am
   B. he is
   C. you are
   D. she is

7. Are Ben and Dave brothers? No, _____ .
   A. they are
   B. he isn't
   C. they aren't
   D. he is

8. Ana has a brother. _____ name is Paul.
   A. Her
   B. Your
   C. His
   D. My

9. Kim and I are married. Lee is _____ son.
   A. my
   B. their
   C. his
   D. our

10. My _____ are tall.
    A. sister
    B. sister's
    C. sisters
    D. brother's

11. My _____ name is Maria.
    A. mother's
    B. brother
    C. mothers
    D. mother

12. My father is not tall. He's _____.
   A. young
   B. short
   C. messy
   D. neat

13. Are Pedro and Alan thin? No, they're _____.
   A. hardworking
   B. tall
   C. heavy
   D. handsome

14. Sally is married to Henry. Henry is her _____.
   A. father
   B. child
   C. uncle
   D. husband

15. My aunt and _____ have two children.
   A. uncle
   B. grandmother
   C. cousin
   D. sister

READING: Look at the school form. Choose the correct answer.

Student's Name					
Last	Tolstoi	**First**	Yuri		
Parent / Guardian					
Name	Sergi Tolstoi	**Relationship**	father		
Address	94 Hilltop Avenue				
City	Arlington	**State**	VA	**Zip**	22207
Telephone #	555-9734	**Work Phone**	555-9255		
Emergency Contact					
Emergency #	555-4562	**Name**	Olga Karpov	**Relationship**	aunt

16. _____ is a student.
   A. Olga
   B. Sergi
   C. Yuri
   D. Tolstoi

17. Sergi is Yuri's _____.
   A. brother
   B. mother
   C. uncle
   D. father

18. Sergi's _____ phone number is 555-9255.
   A. home
   B. school
   C. work
   D. emergency

19. Olga is Yuri's _____.
   A. aunt
   B. mother
   C. teacher
   D. sister

20. Her last name is _____.
   A. Tolstoi
   B. Hilltop
   C. Yuri
   D. Karpov

Lesson 1

1 **LOOK** at the picture. Circle the words that you see in the picture.

map	computer	clock	pencils
notebook	trash can	cell phone	copier
board	chairs	table	books
(desks)	backpack	pens	CDs

2 **WRITE.** What's in the classroom? Write sentences using the circled words in Activity 1. Use *There is* or *There are*.

1. _____There are 3 desks._____

2. _____

3. _____

4. _____

5. _____

6. _____

7. _____

8. _____

3 **CIRCLE** the answer to the questions about the picture in Activity 1.

1. Are there any pencils?　　(Yes, there are)　　No, there aren't.

2. Is there a trash can?　　Yes, there is.　　No, there isn't.

3. Are there any notebooks?　　Yes, there are.　　No, there aren't.

4. Is there a board?　　Yes, there is.　　No, there isn't.

5. Are there any desks?　　Yes, there are.　　No, there aren't.

6. Is there a map?　　Yes, there is.　　No, there isn't.

Lesson 2

1 **WRITE.** Look at your classroom. Write the answers to the questions.

1. How many computers are there? _There are two computers._ _____

2. How many students are there? _____

3. How many desks are there? _____

4. How many windows are there? _____

5. How many doors are there? _____

6. How many chairs are there? _____

2 **CIRCLE** the words in the puzzle.

computer	chair	marker	backpack	clock	floor	closet	bag
board	table	map	notebook	pen	books	door	

R	E	T	U	P	M	O	C	I	T
E	N	E	L	B	A	T	H	O	C
K	K	C	A	P	K	C	A	B	A
R	U	G	I	O	G	L	I	O	M
A	M	A	F	L	O	O	R	A	E
M	I	R	O	O	D	C	P	R	O
B	O	O	K	S	U	K	E	D	R
C	L	O	S	E	T	A	N	E	I
A	E	N	O	T	E	B	O	O	K

Lesson 3

1 **WRITE** *Is there* or *Are there* in the questions.

1. _____*Is there*_____ a meeting room in the library?

2. _____ any computers?

3. _____ a copier?

4. _____ an English class at the library?

5. _____ any books in Spanish?

6. _____ computer classes at the library?

2 **WRITE.** Put the conversation in order.

__4__ B: Are there any videos in the library?

__1__ A: Hello. This is the Washington School Library.

_____ A: OK. What's your question?

_____ B: Great. Thank you very much.

_____ A: Yes, there are hundreds of videos here.

__2__ B: Good morning. I have a question.

__8__ B: How many are in Spanish?

_____ A: Yes, there are more than 500 books on tape.

__6__ B: Are there also any books on tape?

_____ A: You're welcome.

_____ A: There are 200 books on tape in Spanish.

3 **WRITE** answers to questions about the conversation.

1. Is the library in a school? _____

2. What is the name of the library? _____

3. Are the questions about computers? _____

4. How many videos are there in the library? _____

5. How many books on tape are there? _____

6. How many of the books on tape are in Spanish? _____

Culture and Communication — *At the Library*

1 READ AND WRITE. Read the conversation. Use the sentences in the box to complete the conversation.

| a question | thanks | No problem | ~~Excuse me~~ | there are | any computers | 24 |

Anton: (1) _____ Excuse me _____ .

Ms. Davis: Yes?

Anton: Can I ask you (2) _____ ?

Ms. Davis: Sure.

Anton: Are there (3) _____ here?

Ms. Davis: Yes, (4) _____ . They're in the room over there.

Anton: How many are there?

Ms. Davis: There are (5) _____ .

Anton: Oh, (6) _____ very much.

Ms. Davis: (7) _____ .

2 WRITE your own conversation. Use the expressions in the box and your own ideas.

You: _____ .

Ms. Davis: Yes?

You: _____ ?

Ms. Davis: Sure.

You: Is/Are there _____ here?

Ms. Davis: _____ .

You: _____ .

Ms. Davis: There are _____ .

You: _____ .

Ms. Davis: No problem.

Useful Expressions

How to ask a stranger questions

Do you have a minute?

Excuse me.

I'm sorry.

Pardon me.

Can I ask you a question?

I have a question.

Can you help me, please?

May I ask you a question?

Lesson 4

1 WRITE. Use *in, on,* or *at* in the sentences.

1. My office is _____on_____ the first floor.

2. Mark is not _____ work today.

3. He's _____ home.

4. Debbie's backpack is _____ the library.

5. The library is _____ North Street.

6. The school is _____ 822 North Street.

7. Is there a water fountain _____ the second floor?

8. The public telephones are _____ the Townsend Building.

2 LOOK at the building plan. Circle *first floor* or *second floor*.

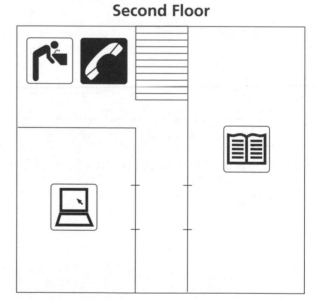

First Floor

Security office

Office

Second Floor

1. The office is on the **first floor** / second floor.

2. The public telephones are on the **first floor** / **second floor**.

3. The snack bar is on the **first floor** / **second floor**.

4. The restrooms are on the **first floor** / **second floor**.

5. The computer lab is on the **first floor** / **second floor**.

6. The security office is on the **first floor** / **second floor**.

7. The library is on the **first floor** / **second floor**.

8. The information desk is on the **first floor** / **second floor**.

Lesson 5

1 **MATCH** the questions and the answers.

__e__ 1. Where's the water fountain?

_____ 2. Is there a snack bar in this building?

_____ 3. Are there any public telephones here?

_____ 4. Where are the restrooms?

_____ 5. Is the office on the second floor?

_____ 6. Are the vending machines in the snack bar?

_____ 7. Where are the computers?

_____ 8. Where is the security office?

a. Yes, it is.

b. No, there aren't.

c. Yes, they are.

d. They're on the second floor.

e. It's on the second floor.

f. It's on the first floor.

g. Yes, there is.

h. They're on the first floor.

2 **WRITE.** Complete the sentences to make questions. Use the words in the box or your own ideas.

vending machine	telephone	classrooms	restrooms

1. Is there a _____ _vending machine_ _____ on the first floor?

2. Are there any _____ on the first floor?

3. Where are the _____?

4. Where is the _____?

5. Is a _____ on the second floor?

6. Are the _____ on the second floor?

7. How many _____ are there on the second floor?

8. _____?

3 **LISTEN** and circle the stressed word or word part.

1. notebook

2. restroom

3. snack bar

4. trash can

5. vending machine

6. water fountain

7. computer lab

8. public telephone

9. security office

10. information desk

11. children

12. backpack

Family Connection — *Open House at School*

1 **LOOK** at the letter and circle the words below.

first floor	library	computer lab	classrooms	teachers
school	second floor	maps	office	

Redding Middle School

Dear Parent/Guardian,

You are invited to Open House night at our school on Wednesday, September 23, from 7:00 p.m. to 9:00 p.m. We have a new computer lab and many new classrooms. Our teachers are here to help you.

There are school maps in the office on the first floor. In the library on the second floor, there are snacks and coffee. Your child's teacher, Mr. Garvin, is in Room 214. There are 20 new computers in the computer lab on the first floor. Come and see them!

Please call 555-2300 for more information.

Sincerely,
The Staff at Redding Middle School

2 **CIRCLE** *yes* or *no*.

1. The name of the school is Open House.   yes   no

2. There is a new office in the school.   yes   no

3. The office is on the second floor.   yes   no

4. There are snacks and coffee in the library.   yes   no

5. The library is on the second floor.   yes   no

6. There are 214 new computers in the school.   yes   no

7. The computer lab is on the first floor.   yes   no

8. The address of the school is 555-2300.   yes   no

9. The Open House night is on September 23.   yes   no

10. Maps of the new computer lab are on the first floor.   yes   no

3 **LOOK** at the floor plan of Redding Middle School. Write the letters of the places. Then complete the sentences.

First Floor:

A [office desk with telephone]
D [stairs]
[gym - person with ball]
C [computer/laptop]
B

Second Floor:

E [open book - library]
F Room 212
G
[table]
H Room 211
I Room 213

1. office __A__
2. library _____
3. computer lab _____
4. Room 214 _____

5. Room 211 _____
6. gym _____
7. stairs _____
8. Room 213 _____

9. The classrooms are _____.
10. The computer lab is _____.

4 **REAL-LIFE LESSON.** Research: What floor is it on? Find these places in your school or your child's school. Write the floor. Find some other places in the building and write them on the list.

Room/Place	Floor
office	*first floor*
restrooms	
library	
computer lab	
water fountains	
vending machines	
my classroom / my child's classroom	
cafeteria	
gym	
auditorium	

Community Connection — *Read a Building Directory*

1 **LOOK** at the directory. Write answers to the questions.

Spadea Center Directory	
Name	**Floor**
Carter, F.	3
Computer Lab	2
Conference Room	3
Halle, M.	2
Information Desk	1
Martin, A.	3
Nguyen, T.	3
Restrooms	2
Snack Bar	1
Supply Room	4
Vending Machines	2

1. Is the computer lab on the first floor?
    No, it isn't. It's on the second floor.

2. Is the Information Desk on the first floor?
    _____

3. Where are the restrooms?
    _____

4. Where is Mr. Halle's office?
    _____

5. Is Ms. Nguyen's office on the second floor?
    _____

6. What is on the fourth floor?
    _____

7. Where are the vending machines?
    _____

8. Where is the snack bar?
    _____

9. Is the snack bar on the same floor as the information desk?
    _____

10. Is Mr. Carter's office on the same floor as the restrooms?
    _____

2 **WRITE** the names of the people, places, and things in the chart.

1st floor	2nd floor	3rd floor	4th floor
Information Desk			

3 READ the conversation. Practice with a friend. Use places from your chart in Activity 2.

> *A:* Excuse me, can you help me, please?
>
> *B:* Sure.
>
> *A:* Where's <u>Mr. Martin's office</u>?
>
> *B:* It's on the <u>third floor</u>.
>
> *A:* The <u>third floor</u>. And, is there <u>an elevator</u> here?
>
> *B:* Yes, there is. There are also <u>some stairs</u> over there.
>
> *A:* Thank you very much.
>
> *B:* It's no problem.

4 REAL-LIFE LESSON. Write what buildings you go to. Are there building directories?

Name of Building	There is a directory.	There isn't a directory.
Community School		✓
Doctor's office	✓	
Shopping mall	✓	
Work		✓

Career Connection — *Ask for Office Supplies*

1 **READ** the phone conversation.

Mr. Haines:	Hello, supply room.
Laura:	Hello. I'm Laura. I have a problem in my office.
Mr. Haines:	Oh? What can I do for you?
Laura:	There isn't a trash can or paper in here. And are there any lamps in the supply room?
Mr. Haines:	I think so. Anything else?
Laura:	Yes, please. Is there a computer?
Mr. Haines:	Yes, there is. I'll bring a trash can, paper, a lamp, and a computer to your office soon.
Laura:	Thank you very much.

2 **CIRCLE** *yes* or *no*.

1. Laura is calling the computer lab.   yes   (no)
2. Mr. Haines is in the supply room.   yes   no
3. There isn't a trash can in Laura's office.   yes   no
4. There are trash cans in the supply room.   yes   no
5. There is a computer in Laura's office.   yes   no
6. There is a computer in the supply room.   yes   no

3 **WRITE** things that Laura needs in her new office. Use words from the box or your own ideas.

computer	copier	telephone	printer
paper	bookshelf	table	trash can

There is...	There are...		There isn't...	There aren't...
1 clock	*2 desks*		*a computer*	
	5 chairs			

Technology Connection: Use Email to Ask for Help

A **LOOK** at Laura's email. Then number the steps in the correct order.

myschool.com

| Check mail | Compose | Search mail | Send | |

(2) Inbox
(1) Draft
(1) Sent
Bulk
Trash

To: GHaines@mycompany.com
From: LDavis@mycompany.com

Dear Mr. Haines,

Thank you for helping me. The computer is great!
Also, are there any bookshelves in the supply room?

Sincerely,
Laura Davis

_____ Click on "send."

_____ Write the email address.

_*1*_ Open "mail."

_____ Click on "new message."

_____ Write your message.

_____ Write the subject.

B **WRITE** an email to Mr. Haines. You have a desk in your new office, but you do not have a clock or a trash can.

myschool.com

| Check mail | Compose | Search mail | Send | |

(2) Inbox
(1) Draft
(1) Sent
Bulk
Trash

To: _____@mycompany.com
From: _____@mycompany.com

Dear _____ ,

Thank you for helping me. The _____
is great! Also, are there any _____
or _____ in the supply room?

Sincerely,

_____

Practice Test

WCD, 18

LISTENING: Listen to the conversations. Then choose the correct answer for each sentence.

1. Which is correct?
   A. The school is on the second floor.
   B. The library is on the second floor.
   C. There isn't a library in the school.
   D. The office is on the second floor.

2.
   A. It's on the first floor.
   B. Yes, there is.
   C. No, there isn't any.
   D. There are five.

3. The woman is looking for _____.
   A. the snack bar
   B. the information desk
   C. library
   D. the public telephones

4. It's in the _____.
   A. West Building
   B. Main Building
   C. Williams Building
   D. School Building

5. It's on the _____.
   A. third floor
   B. second floor
   C. first floor
   D. office

GRAMMAR: Choose the correct word to complete each sentence.

6. _____ there a water fountain?
   A. Am
   B. Is
   C. Are
   D. A

7. _____ there any public telephones in the building?
   A. Am
   B. Is
   C. Are
   D. A

8. There _____ vending machines in the school.
   A. am not
   B. isn't
   C. aren't
   D. no

9. The office is _____ the first floor.
   A. on
   B. in
   C. at
   D. of

10. My backpack is _____ the computer lab.
    A. on
    B. in
    C. at
    D. for

11. Paul and Sara are _____ home.
    A. on
    B. to
    C. in
    D. at

12. The computers are in the _____.
   A. lobby
   B. computer lab
   C. snack bar
   D. restrooms

13. The _____ is at the security desk.
   A. library
   B. nurse
   C. police officer
   D. receptionist

14. There are hundreds of books in the _____.
   A. library
   B. supply room
   C. information desk
   D. hall

15. There are tables and chairs in the _____.
   A. information desk
   B. meeting room
   C. restrooms
   D. stairs

16. There are _____ at the information desk.
   A. classes
   B. water fountains
   C. snack bars
   D. maps

READING: Read the sign. Choose the correct answer.

17. Where's the library? It's _____.
   A. on the first floor
   B. on the second floor
   C. in Room 16
   D. in the computer lab

18. There are _____ on the second floor.
   A. classrooms
   B. computer labs
   C. security offices
   D. snack bars

19. There aren't any _____ on the first floor.
   A. vending machines
   B. computers
   C. classrooms
   D. students

20. The _____ is in Room 16.
   A. public telephones
   B. computers
   C. security office
   D. vending machines

Welcome to Clark Street School	
Information Desk	1st floor
Security Office	1st floor, Room 16
Library	2nd floor
Computer Lab	1st floor, Room 15
Snack Bar	1st floor, Room 12
Vending Machines	1st floor, Room 12
Classrooms 20–29	2nd floor
Public Telephones	2nd floor

Lesson 1

1 MATCH. Match the questions and answers. Write the letters.

_d_ **1.** Is it cold?   **a.** No, it's dry.

_____ **2.** Is it rainy?   **b.** No, it's humid.

_____ **3.** Is it clear?   **c.** No, it's cool.

_____ **4.** Is it warm?   **d.** No, it's hot.

_____ **5.** Is it dry?   **e.** No, it's sunny.

_____ **6.** Is it humid?   **f.** No, it's cloudy.

2 WRITE. Look at the map and write the weather in the cities.

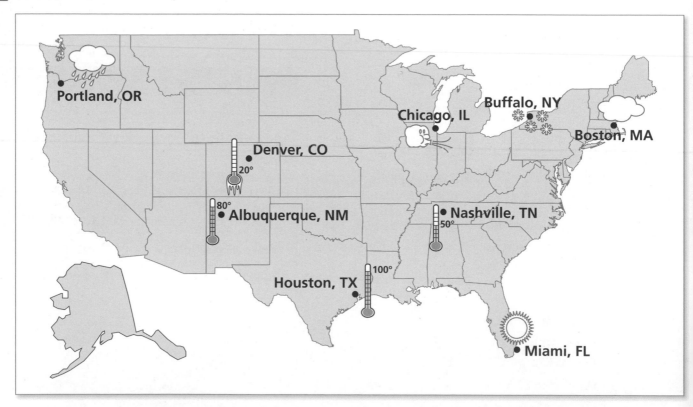

1. In Boston, _____ it's cloudy _____ .   **6.** _____ in Houston.

2. In Buffalo, _____ .   **7.** In Denver, _____ .

3. In Chicago, _____ .   **8.** In Albuquerque, _____ .

4. _____ in Nashville.   **9.** _____ in Portland.

5. _____ in Miami.

Lesson 2

1 READ AND WRITE. Read the letter and complete the sentences. Use the words in the box.

Summer	~~January~~	cool	cold	snowy	hot

(1) _____*January*_____ 15, 2008

Dear Julio,

How are you doing in Los Angeles? Here in Boston, it's winter. It's (2) _____

and (3) _____. I like the snow, but I don't like the cold. I like fall in Boston. It's

(4) _____ and dry. (5) _____ is great. It's (6) _____

and usually sunny.

Write soon. Tell about the weather in LA.

Josefina

2 WRITE the months. Then write the months in order.

A.

1. F B R Y E A U R _____*February*_____
2. B O C O E R T _____
3. R A M H C _____
4. Y A M _____
5. L A I P R _____
6. V O E B E R M N _____
7. S T A U U G _____
8. Y J R A A N U _____
9. L Y U J _____
10. D E M C E E R B _____
11. N E J U _____
12. P T M E R E B S E _____

B.

1. _____
2. _____*February*_____
3. _____
4. _____
5. _____
6. _____
7. _____
8. _____
9. _____
10. _____
11. _____
12. _____

Lesson 3

1 LISTEN AND WRITE. Complete the chart with the weather and the temperature.

City	Weather	Temperature
1. Atlanta	*rainy and* _____	75°
2. Detroit		
3. Salt Lake City		
4. San Diego		

2 WRITE. Complete the conversation with words from the chart in Activity 1.

> A: Hi, Greg! How's the weather in Atlanta today?
>
> B: It's (1) _____ and (2) _____. It's (3) _____ degrees.
> How's the weather in (4) _____?
>
> A: It's (5) _____ and (6) _____. It's 92 degrees.
>
> B: That *is* hot!

3 WRITE. Look at the thermometer and write the missing temperatures. How is the weather? Write *hot, cold, cool,* or *warm*.

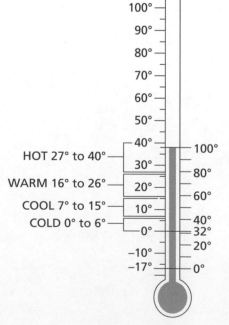

1. 5° C = _41_ ° F   It's _cold_ .

2. _____° C = 50° F   It's _____ .

3. _____° C = 68° F   It's _____ .

4. 30° C = _____° F   It's _____ .

5. _____° C = 100° F   It's _____ .

6. 15° C = _____° F   It's _____ .

7. 0° C = _____° F   It's _____ .

8. _____° C = 0° F   It's _____ .

9. _____° C = 75° F   It's _____ .

10. 37° C = _____° F   It's _____ .

HOT 27° to 40°
WARM 16° to 26°
COOL 7° to 15°
COLD 0° to 6°

Culture and Communication — *Talk About the Weather*

1 LISTEN. Read the conversation.

WCD, 20

Hi, Stan.

Fine. And you?

OK.

. . . ?

Hi, Carmen. How are you?

. . . ?

What do you say now?

Talk about the weather!

It's really *cold* today.

You're right. And it's *windy*, too. *It's terrible weather today.*

Useful Expressions

To talk about the weather
I love this weather!
I hate this weather!
It's great weather today!
It's terrible weather today!

2 READ AND CHECK. Read the sentences. What do you think? Check the type of weather.

	I love this weather.	I hate this weather.	It's great weather.	It's terrible weather.
sunny	✓			
hot				
rainy				
snowy				
cold				
dry				
humid				
cloudy				

3 WRITE. Complete the conversation with your own words. Practice with a partner.

A: It's really _____ today.

B: You're right. And it's _____, too. _____.

Lesson 4

1 MATCH the clocks with the times. Write the letters.

_____ 1. It's four fifteen.   a. 🕐

_____ 2. It's ten thirty.   b. 🕐

_____ 3. It's seven o'clock.   c. 🕐

_____ 4. It's nine ten.   d. 🕐

_____ 5. It's one twenty.   e. 🕐

_____ 6. It's twelve thirty.   f. 🕐

2 WRITE the answer to the question. Use *at* or *in* with the word or time in parentheses.

1. When is the computer class?   (8:00) _____ *It's at 8:00.* _____

2. What time is your class?   (4:30) _____

3. When is your birthday?   (July) _____

4. When is the party?   (evening) _____

5. What time is the meeting?   (10:45) _____

6. When is the test?   (2:15) _____

7. What time are the TV shows?   (8:00, 9:00) _____

8. When are the school holidays?   (December, July) _____

3 WRITE. Complete the sentences with *in*, *on*, or *at*.

1. Carmen's birthday is _____ June 12.

2. There is a big holiday _____ November.

3. Valentine's Day is _____ February 14.

4. The Halloween party is _____ 8:00.

5. Is Independence Day _____ July 14?

6. What holiday is _____ October 31?

7. Is the movie _____ 7:30?

8. Is there a holiday _____ January?

Lesson 5

WCD, 21

1 **LISTEN.** Circle the word you hear.

1. six / sixth

2. eight / eighth

3. twenty / twentieth

4. four / fourth

5. thirty / thirtieth

6. seventeen / seventeenth

7. twenty-five / twenty-fifth

8. nine / ninth

2 **READ** the clue. Write the name of the holiday.

Labor Day	Thanksgiving	Valentine's Day	~~Halloween~~	Independence Day	New Year's Day

1. It's in the fall. Many children like this holiday. It's on October 31. ___*Halloween*___

2. It's in the winter. It's in the first month of the year. It's on the first day of the first month. _____

3. This holiday is also in the winter. It's in the second month of the year. It's the fourteenth of that month. _____

4. This holiday is in the summer. It's hot and sunny in the afternoon. At night, there are many people outside for this holiday. It's on the fourth of July. _____

5. This holiday is in the fall. The weather is cool and windy. It's in November. It's always on Thursday. _____

6. This holiday is in the summer. It's in September. It's on a Monday. _____

Family Connection — *Extreme Weather*

1 **READ AND WRITE.** Read the definitions. Write the correct words under the illustrations.

Storms and Extreme Weather	
blizzard:	very snowy and very windy
hurricane:	very rainy and very windy with winds up to 74 miles (119 km) per hour
tornado:	cloudy and very windy with winds up to 500 miles (800 km) per hour
flood:	too much water after rainy weather

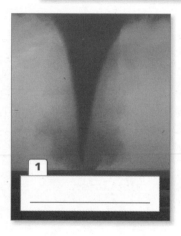

1. _____

2. _____

3. _____

4. _____

2 **CIRCLE** the symbols for the extreme weather.

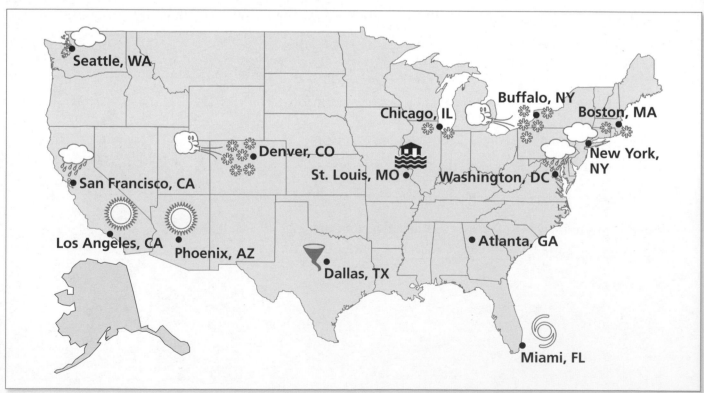

3 **WRITE** answers to the questions about the map.

1. How many blizzards are there? _____

2. Where are the blizzards? _____

3. Is there a flood in Boston? _____

4. Where is there a flood? _____

5. Where is there a tornado? _____

6. Is there a hurricane in Denver? _____

7. Where is there a hurricane? _____

8. Is there bad weather in your city? _____

4 **READ AND WRITE.** Complete the sentences. Use the words in the box.

hurricane	windows	home	~~windy~~	school	weather

Today it is very cloudy and rainy. It is also very (1) _____*windy*_____. My son

always listens to the radio. Today, there's a (2) _____ coming to our city.

We are checking the house before the hurricane. First, the (3) _____ are closed.

We check that everyone is in the house. Then we close the doors. The radio and TV are on.

We listen for (4) _____ reports. There is no (5) _____ today.

We are all at (6) _____, and we're ready for the hurricane.

5 **REAL-LIFE LESSON.** Ask a friend about extreme weather and where to get news or help. What phone number do you call? What radio station or TV station gives you news? Where on the Internet can you get information?

I want to know . . .	Telephone #/Radio/TV/Internet?
1. Is there school today?	
2. Is there a weather problem?	
3. Is there a person to help me?	
4. Where do I go?	
5. _____	

Community Connection — *Weather Forecast*

1 **MATCH** the dates.

_____ **1.** April 20   **a.** 10/27

_____ **2.** June 10   **b.** 5/6

_____ **3.** December 30   **c.** 2/4

_____ **4.** January 12   **d.** 9/22

_____ **5.** October 27   **e.** 6/10

_____ **6.** February 4   **f.** 4/20

_____ **7.** May 6   **g.** 1/12

_____ **8.** September 22   **h.** 12/30

2 **CIRCLE** the dates. Underline the weather words and temperatures.

Today 8/25 Tuesday	8/26 Wednesday	8/27 Thursday	8/28 Friday	8/29 Saturday
Sunny. High around 85°F. Winds 5 to 10 mph.	Partly cloudy. High 76°.	Some rain. High 72°.	Rain in the morning and afternoon. Clearing at night. High 78°.	Cloudy in the morning followed by afternoon sun. High 83°.

3 **WRITE.** Complete the sentences about Activity 2.

hot	rainy	afternoon	morning	cloudy	~~August~~

1. Today is _____*August*_____ 25.

2. It's sunny and _____ today.

3. On Wednesday, it is _____ .

4. It's _____ on Thursday.

5. On Friday, it's rainy in the morning and _____ .

6. It's cloudy in the _____ on Saturday. Then it's sunny.

4 WRITE your own forecast for the next five days. Write the dates. Then write the words for the weather.

Date	Symbol	Weather words	Temperature

5 REAL-LIFE LESSON. Look in the newspaper or on the Internet. Find a weather forecast for another city. Is your weather forecast the same or different?

In my town, the weather is _____.

In _____, the weather is _____.

5 Day Forecast

MON   TUES   WED   ?S   FRI

83   83   85

Career Connection — *Computer Calendars*

1 CIRCLE the short forms for the days of the week that are in Isabel's calendar. Look at the words in the box for help.

~~Sunday~~	Monday	Tuesday	Wednesday	Thursday	Friday	Saturday

November							
	(Sun) **10**	**Mon** **11**	**Tues** **12**	**Wed** **13**	**Thurs** **14**	**Fri** **15**	**Sat** **16**
9:00 A.M.						Office meeting	
10:00 A.M.							Tennis with Pavel
11:00 A.M.							
12:00 P.M.			Lunch/Leyla				
1:00 P.M.							
2:00 P.M.		Holiday		2:45 New boss			
3:00 P.M.							
4:00 P.M.							
5:00 P.M.							
6:00 P.M.							
7:00 P.M.					Birthday Party for Marcos		
8:00 P.M.							

2 WRITE. Answer the questions about the calendar.

1. When is Marcos's birthday? _____

2. What time is Isabel's appointment with her new boss? _____

3. When is the holiday? _____

4. What time is Isabel having lunch with Leyla? _____

5. When is Isabel playing tennis? _____

3 **WRITE.** Look at the holidays and dates. Write the dates using numbers.

1. New Year's Day is January 1.   1/1

2. Independence Day is July 4.   _____

3. Labor Day is September 4.   _____

4. Veteran's Day is November 11.   _____

5. Thanksgiving is November 23.   _____

6. Christmas is December 25.   _____

NOW write the name of the holiday on Isabel's calendar.

Technology Connection: Set an Event on a Computer Calendar

Isabel uses a calendar on her computer. On the calendar, she writes things to do and people to see. She writes notes about important dates like birthdays and holidays.

A **WRITE.** Number the steps for adding an event to a calendar. Look back at the calendar in Activity 1.

To add an event on a computer calendar:

____1____ Write in the name of the person or event.

_____ Choose the day (date).

_____ Pull the cursor down to the time the event ends.

_____ Put the cursor on the time to begin.

_____ Add other notes.

B **READ.** Isabel doesn't want to miss her mother's birthday. She wants the birthday on the calendar every year. It's on November 16. Read the directions for repeating an event. Circle the correct words.

1. Choose **12/16** / **11/16**.

2. Write **"Isabel"** / **"Mom."**

3. Check **"all-week"** / **"all-day"** event.

4. Find **"Repeat"** / **"Trash."**

5. Check **"every day"** / **"every year."**

Practice Test

LISTENING: Listen to the conversations. Then choose the correct answer for each sentence.

1. Which is correct?
   A. It's windy and cold in Atlanta.
   B. It's windy and warm in Chicago.
   C. It's windy and cold in Chicago.
   D. It's 25 degrees in Atlanta.

2.
   A. It's on November 23.
   B. You're right. And it's humid, too.
   C. You're right. And it's cold and snowy, too.
   D. It's not dry today.

3. The holiday is in _____.
   A. the summer
   B. January
   C. February
   D. the spring

4. There is _____ on the holiday.
   A. class
   B. no class
   C. no party
   D. work

5. The party is at _____.
   A. 8:00 A.M.
   B. 8:15 P.M.
   C. 8:00 P.M.
   D. 8:45 A.M.

GRAMMAR: Choose the correct word to complete each sentence.

6. What time is it? _____ four o'clock.
   A. It's in
   B. Is it
   C. I'm
   D. It's

7. When is your class? It's _____ the evening.
   A. on
   B. for
   C. in
   D. at

8. _____ is your birthday?
   A. What time
   B. When
   C. What
   D. Where

9. Halloween is _____ October 31.
   A. on
   B. in
   C. at
   D. by

10. Valentine's Day is _____ February.
    A. on
    B. in
    C. at
    D. for

11. Independence Day is _____ the summer.
    A. on
    B. to
    C. in
    D. at

VOCABULARY: Choose the best word to complete the sentence.

12. It's _____ and cold in the winter.
    A. warm
    B. snowy
    C. hot
    D. dry

13. It's cool and windy in the _____.
    A. spring
    B. summer
    C. Atlanta
    D. holiday

14. It's not cloudy. It's _____.
    A. foggy
    B. humid
    C. rainy
    D. clear

15. It's not dry today. It's _____.
    A. hot
    B. sunny
    C. wet
    D. cold

16. My class is at 7:00 P.M. It's at _____.
    A. night
    B. morning
    C. afternoon
    D. evening

READING: Choose the correct answer.

Andrea Belk	
Thurs., 3/7	
8:00	meeting: Mr. Hossa
10:00	meeting: Peter (supplies)
Noon	lunch with Diana
2:00	meeting: Ms. Ruiz
4:00	
6:00	Dr. Jones
8:00	

17. The date is _____.
    A. March 7
    B. May 7
    C. July 3
    D. June 3

18. It's _____.
    A. Tuesday
    B. a birthday
    C. a holiday
    D. Thursday

19. Andrea has two meetings in the _____.
    A. night
    B. morning
    C. evening
    D. afternoon

20. Andrea has lunch at _____.
    A. 10:00
    B. 11:00
    C. 12:00
    D. 2:00

UNIT **5** In the Community

Lesson 1

1 **WRITE** the places on the map. Use the words in the box.

drugstore	gas station	post office	bank
hospital	supermarket	library	~~apartment building~~

1. apartment building
2. _____
3. _____
4. _____
5. _____
6. _____
7. _____
8. _____

2 **READ** the sentence. Look at the map. Circle *yes* or *no*.

1. The gas station is next to the hospital.   yes   (no)

2. The bank is across from the supermarket.   yes   no

3. The supermarket is between the library and the post office.   yes   no

4. The post office is across from the drugstore.   yes   no

5. The drugstore is between the gas station and the bank.   yes   no

6. The hospital is next to the library.   yes   no

7. The library is between the apartment building and the bank.   yes   no

8. The supermarket is across from the apartment building.   yes   no

Lesson 2

1 **WRITE.** Look at the map on page 62 and write the preposition *next to*, *between*, *across from*, *behind*, or *in front of*.

1. The drugstore is _____across from_____ the post office.

2. The post office is _____ the hospital.

3. The bank is _____ the apartment building and the drugstore.

4. The library is _____ the bank.

5. The apartment building is _____ the bank.

6. The mailbox is _____ the post office.

2 **WRITE** answers to the questions.

1. Where's the bank?   _____It's next to_____ the apartment building.

2. Where's the library?   _____ the supermarket.

3. Where's the post office?   _____ the library and the hospital.

4. Where's the supermarket?   _____ the apartment building.

5. Where's the gas station?   _____ the hospital.

6. Where's the drugstore?   _____ the bank and the gas station.

3 **READ AND WRITE.** Read about the people. Write where they are. Use the words in the box.

~~restaurant~~	fire station	poli<u>c</u>e station	ho<u>t</u>el	super<u>m</u>arket	hos<u>p</u>ital

1. Sara is a server at the _____restaurant_____.

2. Randy is a salesclerk at the _____.

3. Lee is a doctor. She's at the _____.

4. Anton is a police officer. He's at the _____.

5. Katy is a housekeeper at the _____.

6. Ben is a firefighter. He's at the _____.

4 **LOOK** at the underlined letters in Activity 3. Arrange the letters to find out where he is.

Dan is at his __a__ __ __ __ __t__ __ __ __ __.

Lesson 3

1 **LISTEN** to the conversations. Write the letter of the picture.

 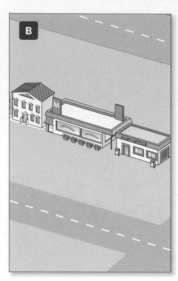 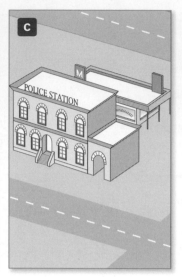 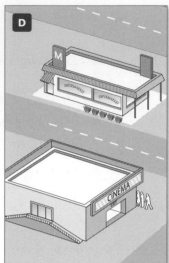

1. _____

2. _____

3. _____

4. _____

2 **WRITE** the questions and answers.

1. supermarket / the / Where's / ?   _____

2. post / It's / office / to / the / next / .   _____

3. the / Where / community / is / center / ?   _____

4. from / across / supermarket / It's / the / .   _____

3 **READ AND WRITE.** Read the conversation. Write the questions and answers from Activity 2.

> *A:* Excuse me. (1) _____?
>
> *B:* (2) _____ .
>
> *A:* Oh . . . (3) _____?
>
> *B:* (4) _____ .
>
> *A:* OK. Thank you.
>
> *B:* No problem. You're welcome.

Culture and Communication — *Ask for More Information*

1 **MATCH** the questions and answers.

_____ **1.** Where's the post office?

_____ **2.** Did you say "Boston Street"?

_____ **3.** How do you spell that?

_____ **4.** Can you say that again?

a. Sure. Boylston Street.

b. No, that's not right. It's Boylston Street.

c. B-O-Y-L-S-T-O-N.

d. It's on Boylston Street, next to the bank.

2 **READ AND WRITE.** Read and complete the conversation. Use the expressions from the box.

Where's the	Thank you	next to the bank	not right	No problem	~~Excuse me~~

A: (1) _____ *Excuse me* _____. Could you help me, please?

B: Sure.

A: (2) _____ post office?

B: It's on Boylston Street (3) _____.

A: Did you say "Boston Street?"*

B: No, that's (4) _____. It's Boylston Street.

A: How do you spell that?**

B: B-O-Y-L-S-T-O-N.

A: OK. (5) _____ very much.

B: (6) _____.

> **Useful Expressions**
>
> *To ask someone to repeat something
> Please repeat that.
> Can/Could you say that again?
> Can/Could you repeat that, please?
> I'm sorry, what did you say?
> Did you say _____?
>
> **To ask someone to spell something
> How do you spell that?
> Can/Could you spell that?
> How is that spelled?

3 **CIRCLE** *yes* or *no*.

1. The person is looking for the post office. (yes)   no

2. The bank is across from the post office.   yes   no

3. The post office is on Boston Street.   yes   no

4. The bank and the post office are on Boylston Street.   yes   no

4 **PRACTICE** the conversation with a friend.

Lesson 4

1 **CIRCLE** the word.

1. **Park / Make** a U-turn.

2. **Turn / Go** straight on Maple Street.

3. **Go / Stop** in front of the apartment building.

4. **Start / Cross** on Elm Street.

5. **Enter / Turn** left on Maple Street.

6. **Cross / Park** 1st Avenue.

2 **WRITE.** Look at the map. Then write the directions from Activity 1 in the correct order.

1. _____

2. _____

3. _____

4. _____

5. _____

6. _____

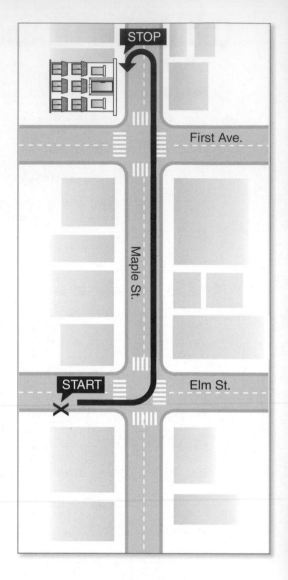

3 **WRITE.** Look at the signs. Complete the sentences. Use *Don't*.

1

_____
in front of the police station.

2

_____
on Pleasant Street.

3

_____
on Central Avenue.

4

_____
on High Street.

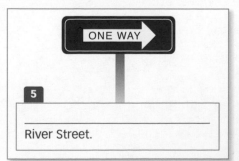

5

_____
River Street.

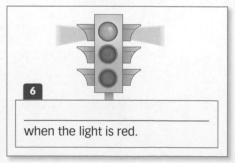

6

_____
when the light is red.

Lesson 5

WCD, 24

1 **LISTEN.** Circle the stressed word or words.

1. Go right on Maple Street.

2. Turn left at the corner.

3. Go straight on First Street.

4. Cross the street.

5. Make a U-turn.

6. Park next to the library.

2 **CIRCLE** the words in the puzzle.

stop	go	~~cross~~	enter	park	U-turn	straight	turn left	turn right

C	R	O	S	S	T	A	M	P	O	F	T
S	E	A	T	R	G	U	O	L	E	U	U
E	T	K	O	M	O	N	R	S	R	G	R
L	E	R	P	U	T	U	R	N	U	A	N
A	N	A	A	P	E	A	R	O	B	H	L
M	O	P	O	I	S	I	T	W	O	I	E
P	E	N	R	K	G	O	S	H	U	R	F
U	T	R	O	H	A	H	I	E	T	G	T
H	E	N	T	E	R	O	T	A	P	S	N

Family Connection — *Emergencies*

1 **READ** the directions. Complete the sentences. Use the words in the box.

right	the stairs	the building	~~the room~~	the door	Go straight

When there's an emergency . . .

1. Go out of _____ *the room* _____.

2. _____ down the hall.

3. Turn _____.

4. Go down _____.

5. Go to the Emergency Exit and open _____.

6. Walk away from _____.

7. Don't go back into the building.

2 **WRITE** the numbers of the directions from Activity 1 in the floor plan.

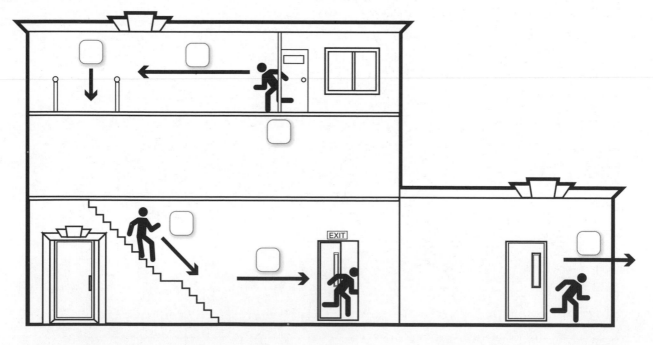

3 **MATCH** the words and their meanings.

_____ **1.** emergency

_____ **2.** exit

_____ **3.** alarm

_____ **4.** away from

a. a bell or buzzer to warn of danger

b. a serious problem (fire, earthquake)

c. not next to; far from

d. the way out of a building

4 READ AND CIRCLE. Read about fire drills. Circle the correct word.

Fire Drills

In (1) **schools / supermarkets**, teachers and students practice what to do in an (2) **exit / emergency**. Here are some of the rules they practice.

1. Look for the list of (3) **people / directions** in the classroom.

2. Study the floor plan of the (4) **room / building** so you know where to go and what to do.

3. Look for emergency (5) **exits / halls** in the building.

4. When you hear the (6) **alarm / fire**, walk to the exit. Don't run!

It's important to follow the directions when there is an emergency.

 5 REAL-LIFE LESSON. Look for emergency exits in your school, office, or home. Complete the chart with information you find.

Place	Emergency Exits	Location
school	2	*next to stairs, beside Room 137*
office/workplace		
home/apartment		

DRAW a map of one emergency exit near you. Draw the map from you to the exit.

Community Connection — *Get a Driver's License*

1 **READ** about Ben. Circle the words to complete the sentences.

Ben is a construction worker. He wants to drive. He needs to get a **driver's license**.

To get a license, Ben needs to

- go to the **Department of Motor Vehicles**,
- fill out an **application**,
- take an **eye test**,
- take a **written** test,

- take a **driving** test,
- get his photo taken,
- and pay $50.

1. A driver's license is for **working / driving**.

2. You get a driver's license at the **Department of Motor Vehicles / police station**.

3. You take **fifty / three** tests.

4. "Turn left at the corner." This is part of the **eye test / driving test**.

5. "When a school bus has flashing red lights, you need to _____."
   This is part of the **written test / driving test**.

6. "Read the letters." This is part of the **written test / eye test**.

2 **MATCH.** Ben is studying for the written test. Match the sign with the meaning.

_____ 1. [H]   a. stop

_____ 2. [walking person]   b. go slow

_____ 3. [pedestrian]   c. let other cars go first

_____ 4. [children playing] d. don't go the wrong way

_____ 5. [SPEED LIMIT 25]   e. hospital

_____ 6. [ONE WAY]   f. people crossing the street

_____ 7. [hexagon]   g. school

_____ 8. [YIELD]   h. playground or park

3 **WRITE** the letters from the driver's license next to the types of personal information.

1. _____ driver's name
2. _____ license number
3. _____ driver's address
4. _____ driver's photo
5. _____ state where the driver lives
6. _____ driver's date of birth

MAINE
WHERE AMERICA'S DAY BEGINS

(A) DRIVER'S LICENSE
(B) 0569243
(C) FIRST NAME: Ben   LAST NAME: Markov
    ADDRESS:
(E) 487 East Street   (F)
    CITY: Portland   STATE: ME   ZIP:
    BIRTHDATE: EXP. DATE:
(G) 09/04/72   (H) 05/30/09
    SEX   HAIR   EYES   HEIGHT   WEIGHT
    M   Br   Br   5'09"   235

(D)

Ben Markov

4 **WRITE.** Complete the license form with your information.

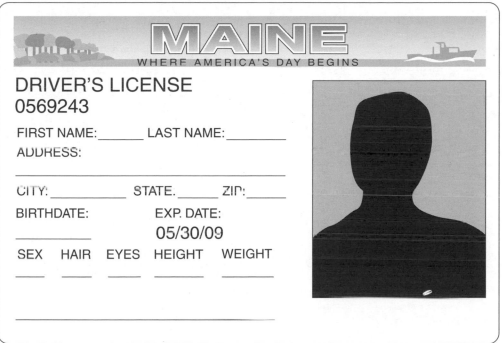

MAINE
WHERE AMERICA'S DAY BEGINS

DRIVER'S LICENSE
0569243

FIRST NAME:_____ LAST NAME:_____
ADDRESS:
_____
CITY:_____ STATE:_____ ZIP:_____
BIRTHDATE: EXP. DATE:
_____   05/30/09
SEX   HAIR   EYES   HEIGHT   WEIGHT
____ ____   ____   _____   _____

_____

5 **REAL-LIFE LESSON.** Ask a friend or read online about the Department of Motor Vehicles in your city.

1. What is the address of the Department of Motor Vehicles? _____

2. What is the telephone number? _____

3. What days and times is the office open? _____

4. Are there practice tests online? _____

5. (Your own question) _____
   _____

Career Connection — *Websites*

1 **READ.** Here is the web page for the community school.

WCS *Welcome to Westside Community School!*
What's your goal? We can help you get there.

- Learn new skills.
- Learn something new.
- Get a degree or certificate.
- Prepare for a new job or career.

We have classes in the daytime, evening, and on the weekend. We have classes at [A] two locations. Some of our classes are [B] online.

We offer courses in:
[C] Accounting
Computer systems
Early childhood education
Nursing and health care

Getting Started
[D] How to Enroll
[E] Tuition and Fees
[F] Frequently Asked Questions

[G] Contact us

2 **CIRCLE** the answers to the questions about Westside Community School.
(NOTE: Some questions have more than one answer!)

1. When are the classes?   ⟨in the morning⟩   ⟨in the afternoon⟩   ⟨in the evening⟩

2. What days are the classes?   **Mon.**   **Tues.**   **Wed.**   **Thurs.**   **Fri.**   **Sat.**   **Sun.**

3. How many locations are there for the classes?   **1**   **2**   **3**

4. Isabel is interested in medical classes. She may take courses in **computer systems / nursing and health care / early childhood education**.

5. Some of the classes are online. You take online courses **at the school / on the computer**.

6. Isabel wants to sign up for some courses. She should click on **How to Enroll / two locations**.

3 READ the course names. Here are some classes. Check the classes for Isabel. She is interested in medical classes.

_____ **1.** English Composition: Improve your writing skills.

_____ **2.** Health Care for the Elderly: Learn how to work with older people.

_____ **3.** American History: How did our country grow and become what it is today?

_____ **4.** Human Biology: How does the body work?

_____ **5.** Human Growth and Development: How do people grow?

_____ **6.** Microbiology: What makes people sick?

_____ **7.** Introduction to Computer Programming: Make the computer work for you.

Technology Connection: Use Links

Using Links to Find Information

In the website for Westside Community School, there are some words that are underlined or in a different color. They are "links." Click on the links. They will take you to other web pages with more information.

WRITE. Look at the website in Activity 1. Write the letter of the link to learn about . . .

_B_ **1.** online classes

_____ **2.** addresses of the schools

_____ **3.** how much it costs or the fees

_____ **4.** how to write or talk to someone about the school

_____ **5.** what accounting classes there are

_____ **6.** questions many people ask

---

4 REAL-LIFE LESSON. Do any schools in your town have online classes? Check the ones you like.

School	Class	Description	
Pond Side College	Accounting and Finance for the Home	Learn how to manage your money	✓

Practice Test

LISTENING: Listen to the conversations. Then choose the correct answer for each sentence.

1. Where does the woman want to go?
   A. the supermarket
   B. Center Street
   C. the library
   D. the Windsor Hotel

2. Which is correct?
   A. The post office is behind the movie theater.
   B. The post office is on Green Street.
   C. The movie theater is between the police station and Green Street.
   D. The police station is between the movie theater and the post office.

3. First, go straight _____.
   A. three blocks
   B. on Oak Street
   C. two blocks
   D. at the supermarket

4. _____ on Oak Street.
   A. Don't turn
   B. Turn left
   C. Turn right
   D. Stop

5. The _____ is between the drugstore and supermarket.
   A. restaurant
   B. library
   C. police station
   D. movie theater

GRAMMAR: Choose the correct word to complete each sentence.

6. The drugstore is _____ from the post office.
   A. across
   B. between
   C. next
   D. behind

7. My apartment building is _____ the bank and the movie theater.
   A. across
   B. in front
   C. between
   D. next

8. Is the school _____ of the library?
   A. behind
   B. in front
   C. between
   D. next

9. Turn _____ on Washington Street.
   A. between
   B. straight
   C. at
   D. right

10. _____ Broadway.
    A. Stop
    B. Cross
    C. Go
    D. Start

11. Don't _____ a U-turn here.
    A. turn
    B. cross
    C. park
    D. make

VOCABULARY: Choose the best word to complete the sentence.

12. Where are the nurses? They're at the _____.
    A. fire station
    B. restaurant
    C. library
    D. hospital

13. Sasha is a server. She's at the _____.
    A. movie theater
    B. community center
    C. restaurant
    D. supermarket

14. _____ the building and go to the second floor.
    A. Park
    B. Enter
    C. Start
    D. Don't stop

15. Don't turn here. _____
    A. Make a U-turn.
    B. Go straight.
    C. Cross the street.
    D. Start on Main Street.

16. How far is it? It's _____.
    A. two blocks
    B. next to the bank
    C. on the second floor
    D. on Main Street

READING: Read the map. Choose the correct answer.

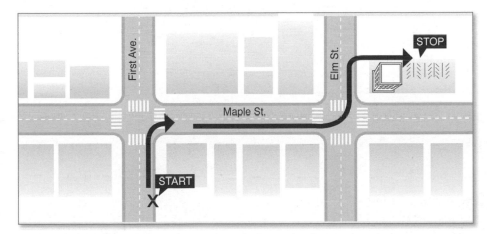

17. Start on _____.
    A. Elm Street
    B. Maple Street
    C. First Avenue
    D. the apartment

18. _____ on Maple Street.
    A. Cross
    B. Turn right
    C. Turn left
    D. Park

19. On Elm Street, _____.
    A. don't enter
    B. make a U-turn
    C. go straight
    D. turn left

20. Park _____ the building.
    A. behind
    B. in front of
    C. across from
    D. next to

UNIT 6 Shopping

Lesson 1

1 **CIRCLE** the correct forms of the verbs.

1. Mai **is** / **are** looking for a new hat.
2. We **is** / **are** talking about the sales clerk.
3. The customers **am** / **are** waiting for some help.
4. I **am** / **are** buying some pants.
5. The salesclerk **am** / **is** helping me.
6. You **am** / **are** shopping for a jacket.
7. She **is** / **are** trying on a dress.
8. We **am** / **are** carrying our books.

2 **WRITE.** Complete the sentences. Use the present continuous.

1. The students _____are talking_____ (talk) to the teacher.
2. You _____ (work) in the community center.
3. The children _____ (wait) for their parents.
4. Mr. Peters _____ (carry) some bags.
5. I _____ (try) on a new jacket.
6. We _____ (help) the children with their homework.

3 **WRITE.** Write the negative form of the verb.

1. Ana **is working** at the hospital. She _____isn't working_____ at the drugstore.
2. Eric and I **are shopping** in the supermarket. We _____ at the drugstore.
3. I **am talking** to Mark. I _____ to Ana.
4. Alex **is looking** for a jacket. He _____ for a computer.
5. My sisters **are waiting** for me. They _____ for my brother.
6. They **are carrying** some books. They _____ the bags.

4 **WRITE** sentences. Put the words in order.

1. shirt / yellow / John / wearing / is / a _____John is wearing a yellow shirt._____
2. black / looking / a / Hector / is / for / hat _____
3. trying / is / on / Hana / shoes / white _____
4. red / I'm / shorts / buying _____
5. pants / They / blue / wearing / aren't _____
6. helping / salesclerk / The / is / customers / the _____

Lesson 2

1 **LOOK AND WRITE.** Look at the picture. Write sentences. What is the person wearing? What is the person doing? Use the words in the box.

~~skirt~~	~~shoes~~	~~shirt~~	shorts	jacket	pants	hat	look for
~~work~~	talk	cell phone	bank	go	new shoes	~~restaurant~~	dress

1. Lei ____is wearing____ _a shirt, a skirt, and shoes_ . _She's working in a restaurant_____ .

2. Rachid _____ _____ . _____ .

3. Alan _____ _____ . _____ .

4. Rita _____ _____ . _____ .

2 **WRITE** the word in the correct place.

~~red~~	~~shirt~~	~~look for~~	pants	black	brown	work	dress
talk	help	shorts	green	orange	shoes	carry	jacket
wait	skirt	white	yellow	shop	buy	blue	hat

Colors		Clothing Items		Verbs	
red		shirt		look for	

Lesson 3

1 MATCH the questions and answers.

_____ 1. Can I help you?

_____ 2. What color?

_____ 3. And what size?

_____ 4. OK. They're over here.

_____ 5. Where are the shoes?

_____ 6. Where's the elevator?

a. Brown.

b. They're between the men's and women's clothing.

c. Yes, I'm looking for a jacket.

d. It's next to the stairs.

e. Medium.

f. Thank you!

WCD, 26

2 LISTEN AND CHECK the size and color.

	small	medium	large
1.			
2.			
3.			
4.			
5.			
6.			

blue	black	white	yellow

WCD, 27

3 LISTEN AND CIRCLE *is* or *isn't*, *are* or *aren't*.

1. We **are** / **aren't** shopping for books.

2. Nina **is** / **isn't** looking for some green shorts.

3. The customers **are** / **aren't** waiting in line for the salesclerk.

4. You **are** / **aren't** buying that purple hat.

5. Ivan **is** / **isn't** carrying the bags.

6. Nina and I **are** / **aren't** working here.

Culture and Communication — *Give Feedback*

1 **READ** the questions. Then write your feedback.

Do you like my hat?

I think _____.

I like my hat. Do you like it?

It _____.

Useful Expressions

To give a compliment
It's really nice.
It's beautiful!
It looks great on you.

To give feedback—not positive
Well, it's different.
It's interesting.
It's OK.

2 **WRITE.** Complete the conversation. Use the words in the box.

| great on you | ~~it's different~~ | I'm buying | the blue dress | It's OK |

A: Kelly, do you like the yellow dress?

B: Well, (1) _____it's different_____.

A: But do you like it?

B: _____.

A: You don't like it. Tell me the truth.

B: No, not really. I like (2) _____.

A: OK, then. (3) _____ the blue dress.

B: The blue dress looks (4) _____.

Lesson 4

1 **WRITE** the amounts.

1. $ _____1.25_____

2. $ _____

3. $ _____

4. $ _____

5. $ _____

6. $ _____

2 **WRITE** *is* or *are* in the questions. Write *It's* or *They're* in the answers.

1. How much ____is____ the blue dress?   ___It's___ $30.00.

2. How much _____ the brown shoes?   _____ $18.00.

3. How much _____ the green pants?   _____ $15.00.

4. How much _____ the white jacket?   _____ $45.00.

5. How much _____ the yellow skirt?   _____ $16.50.

6. How much _____ the red hats?   _____ $8.00.

3 **CIRCLE** the correct word.

1. (This)/ These jacket is extra large.

2. This / These shoes are $28.00.

3. That / Those dresses are pretty.

4. That / Those hats are great!

5. This / These white shirt is $14.99.

6. That / Those customer is waiting in line.

Lesson 5

1 **WRITE** *This, That, These,* or *Those.*

1. _____ shirt is small.

2. _____ shoes are white.

3. _____ shorts are OK.

4. _____ hat is my favorite color.

5. _____ pants are large.

6. _____ shirt is blue.

7. _____ black shoes are on sale.

8. _____ jacket isn't on sale.

2 **WRITE** answers to the questions.

1. What is the date on the check? _____

2. How much money is Emil paying? _____

3. Who is Emil paying the money? _____

4. Who signed the check? _____

Emil La Plante   498
934 Western Avenue
Houston, TX 77017
                                        Date: *Sept. 23, 2009*
Pay to the
Order of _*Glove's Dept. Store*_ $ | *$35.88* |

Thirty-five dollars and 88/100 ~~~~~~~~~~~~~~ dollars

People's Bank   *Emil La Plante*

⑈011644034⑈ 07 3940 0498⑈

3 **WRITE** the amounts in numbers.

1. Eight dollars and forty cents _____ *$8.40* _____

2. Twenty-one dollars and eighty-five cents _____

3. Sixty-six dollars and twenty-five cents _____

4. Fifteen dollars and ten cents _____

5. Thirty-two dollars and fifty cents _____

6. Twenty-nine dollars and eleven cents _____

Family Connection — *Cash or Credit?*

1 **READ AND WRITE.** Read the definitions. Write the words under the pictures.

> **cash:** dollar bills and coins (quarters, dimes, nickels)
>
> **a check:** a small piece of paper that you write on to pay for something
>
> **a debit card:** a card from the bank for getting money or paying for something
>
> **a credit card:** a card from a company for buying something and paying for it later

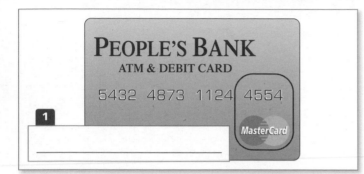

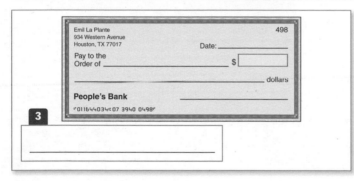

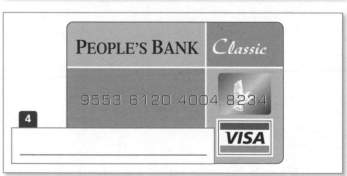

2 **READ AND MATCH.** Emil has $18.37 in his wallet, $485.52 in his checking account, and $1,200.00 available balance (money he can use) on his credit card.

How is Emil paying? Write the letter.

_____ 1. Emil is at the store. He's buying a hat for his son. The hat is $5.95.

_____ 2. Emil is at the drugstore. He's shopping for some things for school and some medicine for his son. It's $27.50.

_____ 3. Emil is at home. He's writing a letter and sending $200 to his sister.

_____ 4. Emil's car is not working. He's at the gas station. The car repairs are $585.

a. check

b. cash

c. credit card

d. debit card

3 **WRITE.** Complete the conversation. Use the words in the box.

Thanks	credit card	checks	cash	~~Are you~~	bag	driver's license

> *Salesclerk:* Is that everything?
>
> *Hung-ju:* Yes, it is.
>
> *Salesclerk:* That comes to a total of $42.39. (1) _____*Are you*_____ paying with
>
> (2) _____ or a (3) _____ ?
>
> *Hung-ju:* Do you accept (4) _____ ?
>
> *Salesclerk:* Yes, if you have a (5) _____ for ID.
>
> *Hung-ju:* OK. Here you go.
>
> *Salesclerk:* Thank you. Here's your receipt and your (6) _____ . Have a nice day.
>
> *Hung-ju:* (7) _____ . You too.

4 **CIRCLE** *yes* or *no*.

1. Hung-ju is at the bank.   yes   (no)

2. Hung-ju is talking to a salesclerk.   yes   no

3. He's paying with a check.   yes   no

4. He is writing "Forty-three dollars and thirty-nine cents."   yes   no

5. He is giving the salesclerk his driver's license, his debit card, and a check.   yes   no

6. The salesclerk is helping Hung-ju.   yes   no

5 **REAL-LIFE LESSON.** Ask a friend about buying things at the different places. How does he or she usually pay? Put a check ✓.

	Cash	Check	Debit card	Credit card
at the supermarket				
at the drugstore				
at the movie theater				
at the post office				
at a restaurant				

Community Connection — *Describe Clothing*

1 **READ AND CIRCLE.** Which one do you like? Circle the word.

1 cheap   expensive

2 in style   out of style

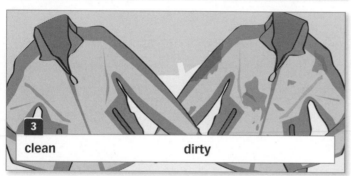

3 clean   dirty

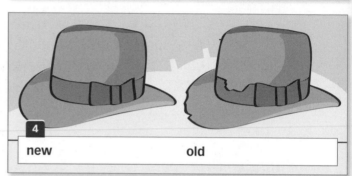

4 new   old

2 **WRITE.** Complete the conversation. Use the words in the box.

| small | ~~white shirt~~ | cheap | on sale | It's | How much is it? | dirty |

A: So, what are you looking for, Kara?

B: A new (1) _____ *white shirt* _____.

A: Here's one. And it's (2) _____, too!

B: It's nice, but it's too (3) _____.

A: Here's a medium.

B: OK. Oh, but look. It's (4) _____.

A: All right. How about this one? It's clean.

B: Maybe.

A: (5) _____ a great buy!

B: Why? (6) _____?

A: It's only $9.98.

B: That's (7) _____! I'll take it.

3 WRITE. Answer the questions about the conversation.

1. What is Kara looking for? _____

2. Is the first shirt too large or too small? _____

3. Is the second shirt too clean or too dirty? _____

4. Is the third shirt cheap or expensive? _____

5. How much is the shirt? _____

6. Does Kara like the shirt? _____

4 WRITE about the clothes in Activity 1.

1	
	The shirt is cheap.

$9.98

2	

3	

4	

5 WRITE about the same clothes. Use the adjective in 1.

1. (expensive) ___*It isn't expensive.*___   3. (dirty) _____

2. (in style) _____   4. (new) _____

6 REAL-LIFE LESSON. Interview a friend. Ask the questions. Write the answers.

1. What's your favorite store? _____

2. Where is it? _____

3. When is it open? _____

4. Why do you like the store? _____

5. Do the salesclerks help the customers? _____

Career Connection — *Write Checks*

1 **READ AND CIRCLE.** Read the words in the box. They are things in Isabel's wallet. Circle the words she uses to buy and pay for things.

(debit card)	driver's license	cash	Social Security card
checks	receipts	credit card	library card

2 **READ.** Isabel is writing a check. Answer the questions about it.

1. Who is Isabel paying? _____

2. How much is the check? _____

3. What is the date on the check? _____

4. Who is signing the check? _____

Isabel Thompson
523 West Street, Apt. 17
My Town, FL 34759   325

Date: *March 28, 2009*

Pay to the
Order of ___*ABC Day Care*___ $ | *$100.00* |

One hundred and 00 cents _____ dollars

People's Bank   *Isabel Thompson*

⑆012345⑆ ⑆123456543⑆ .234567

---

3 **WRITE.** Isabel is paying $650.00 to Milford Realty Company for her apartment. Complete the check for Isabel.

Isabel Thompson
523 West Street, Apt. 17
My Town, FL 34759   325

Date: _____

Pay to the
Order of _____ $ | |

_____ dollars

People's Bank   *Isabel Thompson*

⑆012345⑆ ⑆123456543⑆ .234567

Technology Connection: Use an ATM

A Isabel has $7.50 in cash. She's using her debit card to get money from an ATM (automated teller machine).

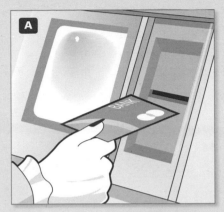

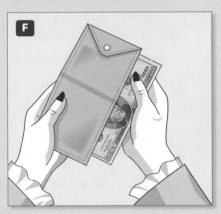

B **READ AND MATCH** the sentences to the pictures.

_____ **1.** I'm counting the cash.

_____ **2.** I'm taking my cash, debit card, and receipt from the machine.

_____ **3.** I'm putting my debit card into the ATM.

_____ **4.** I'm putting the cash in my wallet.

_____ **5.** I'm choosing "$80.00."

_____ **6.** I'm entering my PIN (personal identification number).

Practice Test

LISTENING: Listen to the conversations. Then choose the correct answer for each sentence.

1. What does the customer want?
   A. blue shoes
   B. black pants
   C. black shoes
   D. blue pants

2.
   A. $39.95.
   B. It's too small.
   C. Medium.
   D. Red.

3. The man is _____.
   A. waiting in line
   B. looking for shorts
   C. trying on shoes
   D. helping a customer

4. The woman is _____.
   A. waiting in line
   B. looking for pants
   C. trying on skirts
   D. helping a customer

5. What size is she looking for?
   A. large
   B. thin
   C. medium
   D. small

GRAMMAR AND VOCABULARY: Choose the correct word to complete each sentence.

6. The customers _____ waiting in line.
   A. am
   B. is
   C. are
   D. not

7. I _____ working at the bank.
   A. are
   B. isn't
   C. am
   D. is

8. Rita _____ trying on a skirt.
   A. is
   B. are
   C. am
   D. aren't

9. How much _____ the book?
   A. am
   B. is
   C. are
   D. it is

10. The shoes _____ $24.99.
    A. are
    B. am
    C. is
    D. isn't

11. How much are the _____?
    A. shirt
    B. dress
    C. hat
    D. pants

12. _____ is $5.75.
   A. The shoes
   B. The skirt
   C. The hats
   D. The shorts

13. _____ shirts are on sale.
   A. That
   B. A
   C. This
   D. These

14. I'm buying _____ jacket.
   A. these
   B. some
   C. this
   D. those

15. A _____ is twenty-five cents.
   A. quarter
   B. penny
   C. nickel
   D. dime

READING: Look at the form. Choose the correct answer.

```
        Clothes Mart
     1465 Main Street
         555-7943


Item                    Price

Shirt                  $8.00

Skirt                 $15.00

Jacket                $24.00


       TOTAL      $47.00

   XXXXXXX5543 DEBIT

              $47.00

           03/30/09
```

16. This is a _____.
   A. check
   B. receipt
   C. shopping list
   D. credit card

17. How much is the shirt? _____
   A. eight dollars
   B. eighteen dollars
   C. fifteen dollars
   D. eighty dollars

18. How much are the shirt, skirt, and jacket? _____
   A. four dollars and seventy cents
   B. forty dollars
   C. twenty-four dollars
   D. forty-seven dollars

19. The _____ is on Main Street.
   A. bank
   B. store
   C. customer's apartment
   D. drugstore

20. The customer is paying with _____.
   A. a debit card
   B. cash
   C. a credit card
   D. a check

UNIT **7** Daily Routines

Lesson 1

1 MATCH.

_e_ **1.** Maggie gets	**a.** breakfast at 7:00.
_____ **2.** She takes	**b.** dinner.
_____ **3.** She eats	**c.** a shower.
_____ **4.** Then she brushes	**d.** bed at 10:00.
_____ **5.** At 6:00 P.M. she cooks	**e.** up at 6:30.
_____ **6.** Maggie goes to	**f.** her teeth.

2 CIRCLE the correct form of the verb.

1. Irina and Ana (do) / **does** their homework in the morning.

2. I **work** / **works** from 8:00 to 4:00.

3. Ana **go** / **goes** to school at 1:00.

4. We **cook** / **cooks** dinner at 5:00.

5. They **eat** / **eats** dinner at 7:00.

6. Irina **don't** / **doesn't** read a book after dinner.

7. I **don't** / **doesn't** sleep eight hours at night.

8. We **don't** / **doesn't** get up at 6:00.

3 WRITE. Complete the sentences. Use the correct form of the verb.

1. I _____*work*_____ (work) in a hospital. I _____*don't work*_____ (not work) in a library.

2. Ted _____ (read) books. He _____ (not read) newspapers.

3. Louie _____ (do) his homework in the evening. He _____ (not do) his homework in the morning.

4. We _____ (eat) dinner at 7:00. We _____ (not eat) dinner at 5:00.

5. I _____ (take) a shower in the morning. I _____ (not take) a shower in the evening.

6. She _____ (go) to work at 8:30. She _____ (not go) to work on Saturday.

Lesson 2

1 **WRITE.** Complete the adverbs of frequency. Fill in the missing letters.

1. Dan a __l__ __w__ a __y__ __s__ eats breakfast at 7:00.

2. He _____ o _____ e _____ i _____ e _____ walks to work.

3. He u _____ ua _____ _____ _____ works from 10:00 to 6:00.

4. He o _____ _____ e _____ cooks dinner at 8:00.

5. Dan _____ e _____ e _____ reads at night.

2 **WRITE.** Look at Balbir's schedule. Complete the sentences with *always*, *usually*, *often*, *sometimes*, or *never*.

Sunday	Monday	Tuesday	Wednesday	Thursday	Friday	Saturday
6:30 get up	6:30 get up	6:30 get up	6:30 get up	6:30 get up	6:30 get up	6:30 get up
7:00 exercise	7:00 breakfast	7:00 breakfast	7:00 breakfast	7:00 breakfast	7:00 breakfast	7:00 exercise
8:30 breakfast	8:00–4:00 work	8:00–4:00 work	8:00–4:00 work	8:00–2:00 work	8:00–4:00 work	8:00 breakfast
		4:00–5:00 library		3:00–5:00 library		3:00–5:00 library
6:00 dinner	5:00 dinner	6:00 dinner	5:00 dinner		6:00 dinner	6:00 dinner
	7:00–8:30 class		7:00–8:30 class	7:00 dinner		

1. Balbir ___always___ gets up at 6:30.

2. He _____ gets up at 7:00.

3. He _____ eats breakfast at 7:00.

4. Balbir _____ works from 8:00 to 4:00.

5. He _____ goes to the library in the afternoon.

6. He _____ goes to the library on Sunday.

7. He _____ takes a class in the evening.

8. Balbir _____ eats dinner at 6:00.

Lesson 3

1 **MATCH** the questions and answers.

_c_ **1.** What are you doing?

_____ **2.** At 4:00 in the afternoon?

_____ **3.** Really?

_____ **4.** What's Ali doing?

_____ **5.** At 7:00 in the morning?

_____ **6.** Really? Why?

a. Yes. I often cook dinner at 4:00.

b. Yes. I usually go to work at 7:00, so I cook in the afternoon.

c. I'm cooking dinner.

d. He works from 2:00 P.M. to 10:00 P.M., so he cleans in the morning.

e. He's cleaning the apartment.

f. Yes. He usually cleans in the morning.

2 **WRITE.** Complete the conversation. Use the words in the box.

often	get up	go	~~doing~~	evening	going

A: What are you (1) _____ doing _____ ?

B: I'm (2) _____ to bed.

A: At 8:30 in the (3) _____ ?

B: Yes. I (4) _____ (5) _____ to bed at 8:30.

A: Really?

B: Yes. I (6) _____ at 5:00 in the morning!

3 **WRITE.** Complete the sentences. Use the words in the box or your own ideas.

sleep	~~study~~	work	cook	write
letter	rest	go to the store	play soccer	read the newspaper

1. I always _____ study _____ in the afternoon.

2. I never _____ in the morning.

3. I sometimes _____ in the evening.

4. I often _____ in the morning.

5. I usually _____ in the evening.

Culture and Communication — *Talk about Daily Activities*

1 **LISTEN AND READ.**

WCD, 29

Al: I always eat breakfast. What about you?

Amare: <u>Not me.</u> I'm never hungry in the morning.

Al: I often read the newspaper. What about you?

Amare: <u>Me, too.</u> I always read about events around the world.

Al: I usually cook dinner. What about you?

Amare: <u>No way.</u> I never cook. My brother is a cook.

Al: I always go to bed early. What about you?

Amare: I never do. I do my homework, and then I read.

Al: I usually sleep eight hours a night. What about you?

Amare: I don't. But I always get up and exercise in the morning.

Al: Really? I never do. I hate exercise.

2 **MATCH** the people and the activities. Use the conversation in Activity 1.

___e___ **1.** Al

_____ **2.** Al and Amare

_____ **3.** Amare never

_____ **4.** Al usually

_____ **5.** Amare

_____ **6.** Al never

a. often read the newspaper.

b. cooks dinner.

c. never sleeps eight hours.

d. goes to bed early.

e. always eats breakfast.

f. exercises.

3 **WHAT ABOUT YOU?** Answer the questions. Then write your own questions. Practice with a partner.

1. Do you always eat breakfast? _____*I usually eat breakfast.*_____

2. Do you often read the newspaper? _____

3. Do you usually cook dinner? _____

4. Do you always always go to bed early? _____

5. Do you usually sleep eight hours a night? _____

6. Do you ever exercise? _____

7. I always/sometimes/never _____. What about you?

Useful Expressions
Ways to agree
Me, too.
I do, too.
Ways to disagree
Not me.
No way.

Lesson 4

1 **WRITE** *Do* or *Does* in the questions.

1. _____Do_____ you ride the bus to work?

2. _____ Sara go to school at night?

3. _____ Mark and Paula drive to work?

4. _____ you and I work at 7:00?

5. _____ Paula watch television at night?

6. _____ Mark study in the library?

7. _____ you eat dinner with your family?

8. _____ we play soccer on Friday?

2 **MATCH** the questions and answers.

___f___ 1. Does he always study at home?   **a.** Yes, they do.

_____ 2. Do you take a class in the afternoon?   **b.** Yes, she does.

_____ 3. Does Michelle play soccer on Sundays?   **c.** No, you don't.

_____ 4. Do we take a break at 3:00?   **d.** No, we don't.

_____ 5. Do they leave work at 4:00?   **e.** No, I don't.

_____ 6. Do I work on Wednesday?   **f.** Yes, he does.

3 **WRITE** answers to the questions.

1. Does Alan drive to work?

   Yes, _____ *he does* _____.

2. Does the teacher arrive at 6:00?

   No, _____.

3. Do we take a break at work?

   Yes, _____.

4. Do the children play soccer after school?

   Yes, _____.

5. Do you take a class in the evening?

   _____.

6. Do you walk to school?

   _____.

Lesson 5

1 READ the interview with a famous sports celebrity. Complete the sentences using the correct form of *do* and the verb in parentheses.

Interviewer: (1) Today we are talking to Daniel Buckingham, the famous soccer player. Daniel, _____*do*_____ you _____*play*_____ (play) soccer every day?

Daniel: (2) Yes, I _____. I usually _____ (play) in the morning and afternoon.

Interviewer: (3) _____ you _____ (play) any other sports?

Daniel: (4) Sometimes I _____ (play) tennis or golf.

Interviewer: (5) Tell me, _____ you _____ (eat) any special food?

Daniel: (6) No, I _____. But I _____ (eat) a large breakfast in the morning.

Interviewer: (7) _____ your wife _____ (play) soccer, too?

Daniel: (8) No, she _____. She _____ (work) with music.

Interviewer: (9) _____ you and your wife _____ (eat) at home or in restaurants?

Daniel: (10) Well, we often _____ (eat) at home, but sometimes we _____ (eat) in restaurants.

Interviewer: (11) _____ you and your wife _____ (watch) television?

Daniel: (12) No, we _____. We _____ (read) newspapers and look online for news.

Interviewer: Does your soccer team practice a lot?

Daniel: (13) Yes, we _____. Our team _____ (work) well together, and we _____ (play) a lot. We have a good team, I think.

Interviewer: Well, good luck and thank you.

Daniel: Thank you!

2 LISTEN. Circle *he* or *she*.

1. Does **he** /(**she**)eat dinner at 6:00?

2. Does **he / she** drive to work or take the bus?

3. Does **he / she** come home at 8:00?

4. Does **he / she** work on Fridays?

5. Does **he / she** leave work at 7:00?

6. Does **he / she** take a class at night?

Family Connection — *Help Your Child in School*

1 **MATCH** the words and definitions.

_____ **1.** extra help   **a.** school work or homework

_____ **2.** on time   **b.** take to your house

_____ **3.** stay after school   **c.** a friend or teacher answers questions after class

_____ **4.** assignments   **d.** not leave school after classes

_____ **5.** bring home   **e.** not late

_____ **6.** call on   **f.** ask someone to answer a question

2 **READ AND WRITE.** Read and complete the conversation. Use the words in the box.

answers	after school	~~assignments~~	on time	Does	doesn't	usually	extra help

Mr. Lang: Good afternoon. I'm Mr. Lang. I'm Hetal's teacher.

Ms. Singh: Nice to meet you. I'm Ms. Singh. My son, Hetal, likes your class. Does Hetal have homework every night?

Mr. Lang: Yes, I often give (1) ____assignments____ to do at home. Sometimes Hetal begins the work in class.

Ms. Singh: He doesn't like homework, but he (2) _____ does it.

(3) _____ Hetal talk in class?

Mr. Lang: Well, sometimes. He (4) _____ often ask questions. But he always (5) _____ when I call on him.

Ms. Singh: Does the class use computers in school?

Mr. Lang: Yes, we often do. The students study or write on the computers.

Ms. Singh: Do you stay (6) _____?

Mr. Lang: Yes, I usually do. Some students stay after school for (7) _____. It's a good time for them to ask questions or just review and practice.

Ms. Singh: Thank you. I know that Hetal is sometimes shy.

Mr. Lang: Hetal always arrives (8) _____, and he's a good student. In fact, here's his test from today.

Ms. Singh: Oh, good. Thank you.

3 **CIRCLE** *yes* or *no*.

1. Is Mr. Lang Hetal's father?   yes   (no)
2. Does Hetal do his assignments at home?   yes   no
3. Does Hetal always ask questions in class?   yes   no
4. Are there computers in the school?   yes   no
5. Is there extra help after school?   yes   no
6. Does Hetal arrive late for school?   yes   no

4 **READ** the questions. Check the answers for Ms. Singh. Use Activity 1.

Does ___Hetal___	Always	Usually	Often	Sometimes	Never
like school?	☐	☑	☐	☐	☐
bring school books home?	☐	☐	☐	☐	☐
do his homework?	☐	☐	☐	☐	☐
talk to you about his classes?	☐	☐	☐	☐	☐
study with friends?	☐	☐	☐	☐	☐
call a friend for assignments?	☐	☐	☐	☐	☐
get extra help?	☐	☐	☐	☐	☐
study in the library?	☐	☐	☐	☐	☐
stay after school for extra help?	☐	☐	☐	☐	☐
ask the teacher or a friend for help?	☐	☐	☐	☐	☐
use a computer?	☐	☐	☐	☐	☐
take the bus?	☐	☐	☐	☐	☐
walk to school?	☐	☐	☐	☐	☐
arrive at school on time?	☐	☐	☐	☐	☐
arrive at home on time?	☐	☐	☐	☐	☐

5 **REAL-LIFE LESSON.** Check answers to the questions for your child, another family member, or a neighbor's child. Make a list of how the child can do better in school.

Community Connection — Bus Schedules

1 **READ** the bus schedule. Write the missing times.

Bus 57 Leave Main St.	Arrive Park Place	Arrive Hospital	Arrive Community College	Arrive Central Square
7:15	7:25	7:35	7:50	8:00
8:00	8:10	8:20	8:35	8:45
9:15	9:25	(1) _____	(2) _____	10:00
10:00	(3) _10:10_	(4) _____	10:35	(5) _____

2 **WRITE** answers to the questions about the schedule.

1. What time does the first bus leave Main Street?
   The first bus leaves Main Street at 7:15.

2. Where is the bus at 7:35?
   _____

3. What time does the first bus arrive at Central Square?
   _____

4. Ana takes the bus at 8:00 from Main Street. What time does she arrive at Community College?
   _____

5. John works at Park Place. He arrives at work at 8:30.
   What time does he leave Main Street?

   _____

   _____

6. Oscar leaves Park Place at 10:10. What time does he
   arrive at Central Square?

   _____

   _____

3 READ the conversation. Complete the sentences. Use the bus schedule in Activity 1. The people are on Main Street.

A: Excuse me, does this bus go to Community College?

B: Yes, it does.

A: What time does the next bus leave here?

B: It's 9:10. So the next bus leaves at (1) _____9:15_____ —in about five **minutes**.

A: How long does it take to get to Community College?

B: About **half an hour** . . . (2) _____ **minutes**, to be exact.

A: And how much is the **fare**?

B: It's $1.25.

A: Are there other **stops** on the way?

B: The bus also stops at (3) _____ and at the (4) _____.

A: Is the hospital on the **route**, too?

B: Yes, it is.

A: Thanks a lot.

B: You're welcome.

4 MATCH the words with their meanings.

___d___ **1.** fare   **a.** places where the bus goes to and stops

_____ **2.** minutes   **b.** 30 minutes

_____ **3.** half an hour   **c.** the roads that a bus goes on

_____ **4.** stops   **d.** money you pay for a bus or train

_____ **5.** route   **e.** measures of time; 60 = 1 hour

5 REAL-LIFE LESSON. Interview a family member or neighbor. Ask how he or she gets to work or school. Then write your own question.

1. Do you take the bus or do you drive? _____

2. What time do you leave? What time do you arrive? _____

3. How much is the fare? *or* How much does it cost? _____

4. _____? _____

Career Connection — *Time-Keeping Forms*

1 **READ AND CIRCLE.** Read Isabel's time card. Circle the time that she arrives at work each day. Underline the time that she leaves work each day.

Name: *Isabel*

Period: *Ending July 17*

DATE	Start/In	Stop/Out	Hours Worked
Jul 11	(8:52 A.M.)	<u>4:52 P.M.</u>	8:00
Jul 12	8:57 A.M.	5:02 P.M.	8:05
Jul 13	9:00 A.M.	4:30 P.M.	7:30
Jul 14	8:58 A.M.	4:31 P.M.	7:33
Jul 15	8:55 A.M.	4:29 P.M.	7:34
Jul 16			
Jul 17			

Signature _____

2 **CIRCLE** *yes* or *no*.

1. This is a timecard for June.   yes   (no)

2. Isabel works five days a week.   yes   no

3. Isabel usually arrives at work by 8:00.   yes   no

4. Isabel often gets off work at 4:30.   yes   no

5. Isabel sometimes leaves work at 5:00.   yes   no

6. She always works eight hours a day.   yes   no

3 **CIRCLE** the answer to the question.

1. How many hours did Isabel work this week?
   a. 36 hours and 57 minutes   **b.** 38 hours and 42 minutes   **c.** 45 hours and 7 minutes

2. There is no work on _____ .
   a. July 11–12   **b.** July 16–17   **c.** July 18

3. Isabel gets $9.00 an hour for work. For this week, she gets about _____ .
   a. $72.00   **b.** $500.00   **c.** $345.00

A **LOOK** at the time clock and the swipe card. Write the letter.

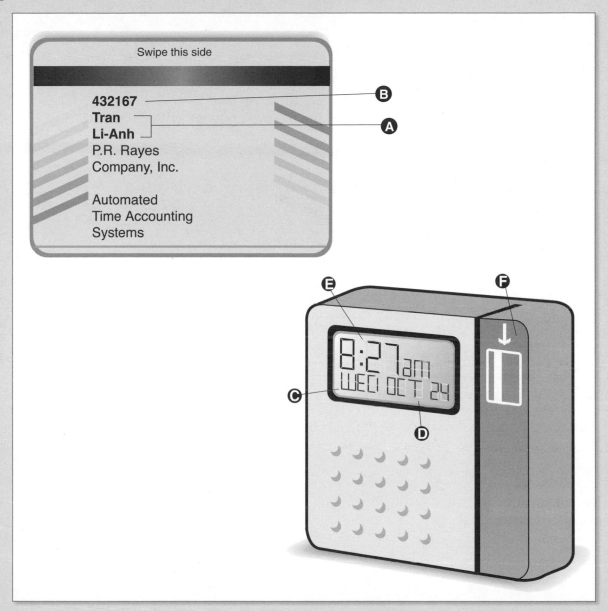

_D_ **1.** Date

_____ **2.** Worker's Name

_____ **3.** Time

_____ **4.** Employee's Number

_____ **5.** Day of Week

_____ **6.** Slide your card here.

Practice Test

LISTENING: Listen to the conversations. Then choose the correct answer for each sentence.

1. Which is correct?
   A. Maria is eating breakfast.
   B. Maria is cleaning the apartment.
   C. Maria's mother is cleaning the apartment.
   D. Maria's mother usually cleans on Thursday.

2.
   A. I leave work at 5:00 P.M.
   B. I sometimes arrive at work at 8:30 A.M.
   C. I usually ride the bus to work.
   D. I usually arrive at work at 9:00 A.M.

3. Pam _____ to work.
   A. walks
   B. drives
   C. takes the bus
   D. arrives late

4. She usually goes home at _____.
   A. 2:30
   B. 4:00
   C. 5:20
   D. 4:30

5. Bill's car is _____.
   A. at the gas station
   B. at home
   C. at work
   D. working

GRAMMAR AND VOCABULARY: Choose the correct word to complete each sentence.

6. Jim always _____ his teeth in the morning.
   A. brush
   B. brushes
   C. does
   D. takes

7. I _____ breakfast at 7:00.
   A. eating
   B. eats
   C. eat
   D. do

8. We _____ work on Saturdays.
   A. do
   B. don't
   C. doesn't
   D. aren't

9. _____ Hector usually cook dinner?
   A. Are
   B. Is
   C. Do
   D. Does

10. _____ Sam and Ellen ride the bus?
    A. Are
    B. Do
    C. Is
    D. Does

11. I call my family every night. I _____ call my family.
    A. always
    B. never
    C. sometimes
    D. often

12. We study on Sunday afternoon and Thursday evening. We _____ study.
    A. sometimes
    B. never
    C. always
    D. don't

13. Do you work at night? Yes, I _____.
    A. am
    B. do
    C. are
    D. does

14. My sister _____ to bed at 9:00.
    A. does
    B. goes
    C. go
    D. gets up

15. I don't ride the bus. I _____ to school.
    A. go
    B. watch
    C. walk
    D. get

READING: Look at the card. Choose the correct answer.

Name: _Chu Peng_

Period: _Ending Feb 17_

DATE	Start/In	Stop/Out	Hours Worked
Feb 10	12:59 P.M.	4:32 P.M.	3:33
Feb 11	12:55 P.M.	4:02 P.M.	3:07
Feb 12	10:00 A.M.	1:30 P.M.	3:30
Feb 14	12:59 P.M.	4:31 P.M.	3:31
Feb 15	12:58 P.M.	4:35 P.M.	3:37
Feb 16			
Feb 17			
Signature			

16. This is _____.
    A. a time card
    B. a work schedule
    C. a class schedule
    D. an employee card

17. What time does Chu usually arrive? _____
    A. 3:30
    B. 1:00
    C. 4:30
    D. 10:00

18. Chu usually works _____
    A. in the afternoon.
    B. at night.
    C. in the morning.
    D. all day.

19. Chu works _____ days a week.
    A. 7
    B. 1 or 2
    C. 3 or 4
    D. 5

20. Chu usually _____ around 4:30.
    A. arrives at work
    B. takes a break
    C. leaves work
    D. works

Lesson 1

1 **WRITE.** Look at the picture. Write the letter of the food.

 A

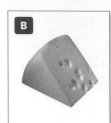 B

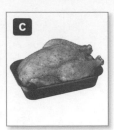 C

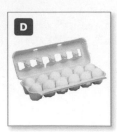 D

 E

 F

 G

 H

 I

 J

 K

 L

_H_ **1.** banana   _____ **5.** cheese   _____ **9.** broccoli

_____ **2.** bread   _____ **6.** chicken   _____ **10.** apple

_____ **3.** carrot   _____ **7.** fish   _____ **11.** onion

_____ **4.** eggs   _____ **8.** orange   _____ **12.** rice

2 **WRITE** *a* or *an* before count nouns. Write "—" before non-count nouns.

1. _an_ onion   **5.** _____ apple   **9.** _____ carrot

2. _____ banana   **6.** _____ rice   **10.** _____ milk

3. _____ bread   **7.** _____ egg   **11.** _____ cheese

4. _____ cereal   **8.** _____ yogurt   **12.** _____ broccoli

3 **WRITE.** Complete the sentences with *is* or *are*.

1. Apples _are_ my favorite fruit.

2. Broccoli _____ a green vegetable.

3. Bananas _____ good for you.

4. These eggs _____ for breakfast.

5. This cheese _____ from France.

6. Rice _____ easy to cook.

7. Chicken _____ not expensive this week.

8. The onions _____ next to the carrots.

Lesson 2

1 MATCH.

_d_ **1.** I always buy a box of

_____ **2.** We eat a loaf of

_____ **3.** I drink a bottle of

_____ **4.** For dinner, Enrique buys two pounds of

_____ **5.** There's a carton of

_____ **6.** Please buy a bag of

a. juice in the afternoon.

b. fish.

c. oranges.

d. cereal.

e. bread at dinner.

f. milk in the kitchen.

2 WRITE. Complete the sentences with a word in the box.

loaf	bag	~~pounds~~	bottle	carton	boxes

Mai is at the supermarket. First, she looks at the vegetables. She buys two (1) _____pounds_____ of broccoli. The fruit is next to the vegetables, so she takes a (2) _____ of oranges. She gets a (3) _____ of bread for sandwiches. Mai also gets two (4) _____ of cereal for breakfast. She buys a (5) _____ of milk, too. Mai takes a (6) _____ of juice to drink. She usually gets apple juice. It's her favorite.

3 READ AND WRITE. Read the sentences. Then write the words.

1. Oranges and onions are in bags. I buy milk in cartons, but I buy a __l__ __o__ __a__ | f | of bread.

2. This is next to the milk in the supermarket. It's usually white, but sometimes there is fruit in it. ____ ____ ____ ____ | | ____

4. I buy cereal in a box. I get a bottle of juice. I buy a ____ ____ | | ____ ____ of fruit or meat.

3. This is a white grain. It's very small and thin. ____ | | ____ ____

5. This is a vegetable. It's orange. It's long and thin. ____ ____ ____ ____ ____ | |

READ the letters in the boxes. What type of food is it? ____ ____ ____ ____

Lesson 3

1 **WRITE.** Complete the conversation. Use the words in the box.

| aisle | How much | on sale | ~~buy~~ | Where | a pound |

A: Let's (1) _____ buy _____ some broccoli. It's (2) _____.

B: (3) _____ is it?

A: $1.19 (4) _____.

B: Sounds good. (5) _____ is it?

A: In (6) _____ 2.

B: Do you buy broccoli every week?

A: Not always. But I like it, and it's good for you.

2 **MATCH** the questions and answers.

__g__ 1. How much is the rice?   **a.** It's $2.75 a box.

_____ 2. How much are the apples?   **b.** The red ones are $1.85 a bag.

_____ 3. How much is the bread?   **c.** They're $1.19 a pound.

_____ 4. How much is the orange juice? **d.** It's $2.25 a carton.

_____ 5. How much are the carrots?   **e.** It's $2.99 a pound.

_____ 6. How much is the cereal?   **f.** It's $1.75 a bottle.

_____ 7. How much is the milk?   **g.** It's $4.29 a bag.

_____ 8. How much is the chicken?   **h.** It's $2.19 a loaf.

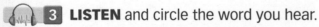

3 **LISTEN** and circle the word you hear.

WCD, 32

1. it   eat   **5.** mitt   meat

2. sit   seat   **6.** chick   cheek

3. chip   cheap   **7.** fit   feet

4. bit   beat   **8.** pick   peek

Culture and Communication—*Would you like…?*

1 **LISTEN AND READ** the conversations.

A: <u>Would you like</u> something to drink?
B: Yes, please.

A: <u>Do you want</u> some juice?
B: No, thank you.

Useful Expressions

Ways to offer

Would you like some/more/a/an ____?

Do you want some/more/a/an ____?

Can I get you some/more/a/an ____?

Would you like anything to drink/eat?

What would you like?

Useful Expressions

Ways to accept or refuse

Accept	Refuse
Yes, please.	No, thank you.
Yes, thanks.	No, thanks.
Thank you.	Nothing for me, thank you.

2 **WRITE.** Complete the conversation.

Al: Would you (1) _____ *like* _____ some <u>chicken</u>?

You: Yes, (2) _____ .

Al: What (3) _____ you like—some <u>broccoli</u> or some <u>carrots</u>?

You: Some (4) _____ , please.

Al: Do you (5) _____ some <u>coffee</u>?

You: No, (6) _____ .

Al: Can I (7) _____ you something to drink?

You: Maybe some <u>juice</u>, (8) _____ .

3 **WHAT ABOUT YOU?** Practice the conversation with a partner. Use other foods.

Lesson 4

1 **WRITE** the prices.

1. Soup is _____$2.00_____.

2. Pie is _____.

3. A hot dog is _____.

4. A sandwich is _____.

5. French fries are _____.

6. Soda is _____.

7. Ice cream is _____.

8. A hamburger is _____.

9. Salad is _____.

2 **MATCH** the questions and answers.

__e__ 1. Where do you buy pie?

_____ 2. When does Mark usually eat soup?

_____ 3. What do you usually eat for dinner?

_____ 4. What do they order for lunch?

_____ 5. When do you usually eat ice cream?

_____ 6. Where do they eat dinner?

a. Chicken and rice.

b. At home.

c. Sandwiches.

d. For lunch.

e. At the supermarket.

f. After dinner.

3 **WRITE** *What*, *Where*, or *When*. Then write *do* or *does*.

1. ____Where____ ____does____ Luis eat lunch?   At work.

2. _____ _____ you usually order for dinner?   Fish and salad.

3. _____ _____ they usually eat ice cream?   After dinner.

4. _____ _____ Peter get fruit?   At the supermarket.

5. _____ _____ you drink in the morning?   Coffee and orange juice.

6. _____ _____ Daniela eat soup?   For lunch.

4 READ AND CIRCLE. Read the conversation. Circle the correct word.

A: Hey, Felipe, what's for dinner?

B: Chicken and rice.

A: Great! What do we (1) **need** / **want** at the grocery store?

B: Let me look in the (2) **grocery store** / **kitchen**. We (3) **have** / **want** chicken in the refrigerator. But we don't (4) **need** / **have** any milk.

A: So how much do we (5) **need** / **have**?

B: Buy a (6) **quart** / **pound** of milk and half a (7) **cup** / **pound** of cheese.

A: What about eggs?

B: You can get a (8) **dozen** / **gallon** eggs, too.

A: Anything else?

B: Oh, we don't (9) **want** / **have** any salt or juice.

A: OK. I'll get some salt and two (10) **ounces** / **quarts** of juice.

---

5 MATH. Read the recipe. Change the measurements.

Cream of Chicken Soup

1. Carrots: (8 ounces) = ___1/2___ pound
2. Onions: (1/2 quart) = _____ cups
3. Celery: (8 ounces) = _____ pound
4. Flour: (1 pound) = _____ ounces
5. Chicken stock, hot: (16 pints) = _____ gallons
6. Milk, hot: (8 pints) = _____ quarts
7. Light cream: (4 cups) = _____ quart
8. Butter: (32 tablespoons) = _____ oz. = _____ pound
   Chicken: 1/2 ounce per serving

Family Connection — *Healthy Eating*

1 LOOK AND CIRCLE. Look at the food pyramid. Circle how much of each category you need every day.

grains
6 oz.

vegetables
2 1/2 cups

fruit
1 1/2 cups

meat and other proteins
5 1/2 oz.

milk (dairy products)
3 cups

oils

2 WRITE the foods in the correct group.

apple	banana	~~bread~~	broccoli	carrot	cereal	cheese	chicken
egg	fish	French fries	hamburger	hot dog	ice cream	milk	onion
orange	pie	rice	salad	soda	yogurt		

Grains	Vegetables	Fruit	Milk (Dairy Products)	Meat and Other Proteins	Other
bread					

3 WRITE answers to the questions.

1. Hana drinks a cup of milk every morning and in the evening. She also has a cup of yogurt in the afternoon. She eats a cheese sandwich for lunch. Does she eat enough from the milk group? _____ Yes, she does. _____

2. Ivan doesn't like oranges. What are some other fruits he can eat? _____

3. Carol has cereal with bananas and milk for breakfast. She has a cheese sandwich and a salad for lunch. She needs more _____.

4. Jeff makes soup. He uses chicken, rice, onions, carrots, and cream. What food group is not in the soup? _____

5. Michelle doesn't eat fish. What other proteins can she eat? _____

6. Oscar doesn't like cheese or yogurt. What does he need? _____

4 **READ AND WRITE.** Read and complete the conversation between Mrs. Lee and her son, Peter. Use names of the food groups.

Mrs. Lee: So, you aren't eating the broccoli and carrots.

Peter: Mom, I don't like them.

Mrs. Lee: But you still need to eat your (1) _____ *vegetables* _____.

Peter: OK.

Mrs. Lee: Do you want some more rice?

Peter: Why not French fries?

Mrs. Lee: French fries aren't very good for you. Rice is a good (2) _____.

Peter: What's for dessert?

Mrs. Lee: Dessert? No. First, eat your fish.

Peter: Why don't we eat hot dogs every night? I like them.

Mrs. Lee: You need different types of (3) _____. It's good for you. Now, drink your milk.

Peter: My friend Andy drinks soda for dinner.

Mrs. Lee: Well, (4) _____ is good for you. What do you want for dessert—an apple or an orange?

Peter: (5) _____? No ice cream? No pie? I want to go to Andy's house!

5 **REAL-LIFE LESSON.** Write the food you eat. Do you eat enough of the different food groups?

FOOD	Grains	Vegetables	Fruit	Milk (Dairy Products)	Meat and Other Proteins	Activity
What You Need	6 oz. (1 oz. grain = 1 slice of bread, 1 cup cereal, 1/2 cup rice or pasta)	2 1/2 cups	1 1/2 cups	3 cups (1 cup milk = 1 cup milk, 1 cup yogurt, 1 1/2 oz. cheese)	5 1/2 oz. (1 oz. = 1 oz. meat, chicken, or fish; 1 egg)	30 to 60 minutes of exercise
Breakfast	*1 oz.*				*1/2 cup*	
Lunch						_____ minutes of exercise
Dinner						
Total						

Community Connection — *Weights and Measures*

1 **MATCH** the measurements and abbreviations.

_f_	**1.** gallon	**a.**	c.
____	**2.** quart	**b.**	oz.
____	**3.** pound	**c.**	tbs.
____	**4.** ounce	**d.**	qt.
____	**5.** cup	**e.**	tsp.
____	**6.** pint	**f.**	gal.
____	**7.** tablespoon	**g.**	lb.
____	**8.** teaspoon	**h.**	pt.

2 **CIRCLE** the weights and measurements.

1

Wild Rice

Nutrition Facts

Serving Size: $\frac{1}{4}$ cup dry
Servings per Package: 2
Ingredients: Wild Rice
Net Wt. 4 oz.

2

CHOCOLATE PUDDING

Net Wt. 3.9 oz.   Four $\frac{1}{2}$ cup servings

NUTRITION FACTS

Serving Size: $\frac{1}{4}$ package
Servings per Package: 4

Directions: Beat pudding mix into 2 c. cold milk for 2 minutes. Pour into dishes. It's ready to eat in 5 minutes.

3

P & M Pasta

Nutrition Facts

Serving Size: 2 oz. (about $\frac{1}{4}$ cup)

Directions for One Pound:
Each pound of pasta (16 oz.) yields about 8 cups cooked or 8 servings.
Heat 5 qts. of water and 1 tbs. salt to a boil.
Stir in pasta.
Boil uncovered 6-8 minutes. Stir occasionally.
Drain well. Toss with 2 tbs. oil, butter, or margarine.

4

TOMATO SOUP

Net Wt. 10 $\frac{3}{4}$ oz.

Nutrition Facts

Serving Size: $\frac{1}{2}$ cup
Servings per Can: 3

Directions: Mix soup + 1 can water.
Heat, stirring occasionally.

3 **WRITE** the answers to the questions.

1. Does the rice weigh 2.5 ounces? _____ No. _____

   How much does it weigh? _____ It weighs 4 ounces. _____

2. How many cups of milk do you need for the chocolate pudding? _____

3. How many cups of pasta does one pound make? _____

4. Do you use milk to make the tomato soup? _____

   What do you use? _____

4 **READ** the conversation. Complete the sentences. Use the information in Activity 2.

> A: What are you doing?
>
> B: I'm making some pudding for dessert.
>
> A: Do you need some help?
>
> B: Sure. I'm making pudding for eight people.
>
> A: This package makes (1) ___4___ servings. So, we need to make (2) _____ packages.
>
> B: Great. How much milk do we need?
>
> A: (3) We need _____ cups for one package, so that's (4) _____ cups.
>
> B: This is easy.
>
> A: It tastes good, too.

5 **REAL-LIFE LESSON.** Look at three food containers at home or in the supermarket. Answer the questions.

	Food #1:	Food #2:	Food #3:
How much does it weigh? (oz., lbs.)			
How much is a serving? (cup)			
What do you need to prepare it?			

Career Connection — *Plan Food and Drinks*

1 CIRCLE the correct word.

1. There's a meeting tomorrow **evening** / (**morning**) at 8:30 A.M. for 20 people.

2. Isabel plans **breakfast** / **lunch** for them.

3. She buys 3 **quarts** / **pints** of orange juice.

4. She buys 3 large **bags** / **boxes** of cereal.

5. She doesn't buy **coffee** / **bread** and tea. There is always some at work.

6. Isabel likes **vegetables** / **fruit** for breakfast.

2 WRITE. Look at the list. Write the types of drinks, food, and other things.

sugar	coffee	cereal	milk	~~tea~~
spoons	yogurt	plates	cream cheese	jam
bowls	fruit	orange juice	knives	bread

Drinks	Food	Other
tea		

3 **WRITE** the letter of the parts of the scale.

___C___ **1.** weight

_____ **2.** price you pay

_____ **3.** price for a pound

_____ **4.** place you put fruit or vegetables

_____ **5.** weight and price display

4 **WRITE.** Number the steps for using the scales.

_____ Choose "onions."

___1___ Put the onions on the scale.

_____ Check the price/pound ($/lb) and total price ($).

_____ Choose the food group "vegetables."

_____ Take the onions off the scale.

Unit 8 Test

WCD, 34

LISTENING: Listen to the conversations. Then choose the correct answer for each sentence.

1.
   A. Great.
   B. Sounds good.
   C. Yes. They're $2.25 a bag.
   D. Let's buy some oranges.

2.
   A. I like them.
   B. In aisle 2.
   C. Where do you get oranges?
   D. I get a sandwich.

3. When do they eat lunch at work?
   A. at 12:00
   B. at 11:30
   C. in the morning
   D. at 2:00

4. Where does Margot eat sometimes?
   A. at home
   B. in a restaurant
   C. in the supermarket
   D. in her office

5. What does she like to eat?
   A. a hamburger and soup
   B. vegetables
   C. a sandwich and French fries
   D. vegetable soup

GRAMMAR AND VOCABULARY: Choose the correct word to complete each sentence.

6. _____ is good for you.
   A. Onions
   B. Eggs
   C. Broccoli
   D. Carrots

7. _____ are in aisle 1.
   A. Bread
   B. Apples
   C. Rice
   D. Milk

8. I like _____.
   A. apple
   B. milk
   C. onion
   D. banana

9. How much is the _____?
   A. chicken
   B. apples
   C. oranges
   D. carrots

10. The _____ are $1.29 a pound.
    A. rice
    B. fish
    C. broccoli
    D. onions

11. There's a _____ of milk in the kitchen.
    A. pound
    B. bag
    C. carton
    D. loaf

12. I buy a _____ of bread every week.
    A. box
    B. loaf
    C. bottle
    D. bag

13. _____ do you eat for dinner? I usually eat chicken and rice.
    A. What
    B. Where
    C. When
    D. How

14. _____ does Maria buy bread? Does she go to the supermarket?
    A. What
    B. Where
    C. When
    D. How

15. _____ do they eat lunch? I eat at 11:30.
    A. What
    B. Where
    C. When
    D. How

READING: Read the card. Then choose the correct answer.

Farmer Style Omelet
(Makes 4 servings)

12 Eggs	4 oz. Potatoes	6 oz. Butter
1/4 c. Milk	1/4 tsp. Salt	1/4 c. Grated cheese
4 oz. Onion	Pepper to taste	

1. Mix the eggs, milk, salt, and pepper.
2. Cook the onions and potatoes in the butter until brown.
3. Pour the eggs and milk over the onions and potatoes. Cook it on the stove.
4. Then put it in the oven to finish.
5. Add cheese on top.

16. This is a _____.
    A. menu
    B. shopping list
    C. recipe
    D. food label

17. How many eggs do you need?
    A. 4 dozen
    B. 1/2 dozen
    C. 8 dozen
    D. 1 dozen

18. You need _____ cup of milk.
    A. 4
    B. 1
    C. 1/2
    D. 1/4

19. How much salt do you need?
    A. 1 tablespoon
    B. 1/4 tablespoon
    C. 1 teaspoon
    D. 1/4 teaspoon

20. You put the _____ last on the omelet.
    A. cheese
    B. salt
    C. butter
    D. pepper

Lesson 1

1 **WRITE.** Complete the sentences. Use the words in the box.

~~server~~	construction worker	taxi driver	salesclerk	office assistant	cook

1. A _____server_____ can take food orders.

2. A _____ can use a cash register.

3. A _____ can prepare meals.

4. A _____ can take measurements and use power tools.

5. An _____ can use a fax machine.

6. A _____ can drive people in a car.

2 **WRITE.** Complete the sentences with *can* or *can't*.

1. Eduardo likes to prepare food. He _____*can*_____ cook.

2. Lise and Stephan are from France. They _____ speak French.

3. Olga is a teacher. She _____ fix teeth.

4. Hung-ju likes to make houses. He _____ use power tools.

5. Paula doesn't like to make dresses. She _____ take measurements.

6. Marcos and Pierre are servers. They _____ take food orders.

7. I'm a construction worker. I _____ drive a forklift.

8. My sister is a receptionist. She _____ fix a car.

3 **MATCH** the questions and answers.

___e___ 1. Can Tom speak Spanish?
_____ 2. Can Fran fix a copier?
_____ 3. Can you read English?
_____ 4. Can you use power tools?
_____ 5. Can you drive a taxi?
_____ 6. Can they use a cash register?
_____ 7. Can he prepare food?
_____ 8. Can she use a fax machine?

a. No, he can't. He doesn't like to cook.
b. Yes, I can. I love books.
c. No, I can't. I don't like to drive.
d. Yes, they can. They work in a store.
e. Yes, he can. He studies Spanish.
f. Yes, she can. She can use a copier, too.
g. Yes, I can. I like to make things.
h. No, she can't. She doesn't like machines.

Lesson 2

1 **WRITE.** Look at the picture. Complete the sentences. Use the words in the box.

electrician	power tools	plumber	water pipes	carpenter
mechanic	wires	~~cabinets~~	toilet	trucks

Mateo

Mark

Halil

Vera

Vera's friends have many different jobs. They are helping her at her new house. Mateo Jiménez is in the kitchen. He can make and fix (1) _____*cabinets*_____ . He can use (2) _____ . He's a (3) _____ . Mark Greene is in the bathroom fixing a (4) _____ . Mark is a (5) _____ . He can also fix the (6) _____ . Halil Burak is in the in the living room. He's an (7) _____ . He's fixing the (8) _____ . Vera isn't in the house. She's outside. She can fix cars and (9) _____ . She's a (10) _____ .

2 **WRITE AND MATCH.** Unscramble the words. Then match the jobs to the skills.

___*f*___ 1. A _____*server*_____ can   **a.** fix _____ .
          vesrre   **crtkus**

_____ 2. A _____ can   **b.** use _____ .
          blemurp   **owpre solot**

_____ 3. A _____ can   **c.** fix _____ .
          petcerinitos   **atrew sipep**

_____ 4. A _____ can   **d.** use a _____ .
          pearternc   **xfa chamien**

_____ 5. A _____ can   **e.** fix _____ .
          chanicme   **weisr**

_____ 6. An _____ can   **f.** take __*food orders*__ .
          tricelianec   **odof sderor**

Lesson 3

WCD, 35

1 **LISTEN** and check the word you hear.

	can	can't	
1. Eva		✓	fix the wires.
2. She			use power tools.
3. Marcos			drive a truck.
4. He			drive a forklift.
5. We			use a computer.
6. We			prepare Chinese food.
7. My brothers			work at night.
8. They			work Saturdays.

2 **WRITE.** Arrange the conversation in order.

_____ *A:* Oh. Do you have any skills?

_____ *A:* That's good. Can you use a fax machine?

___1___ *A:* What kind of job are you looking for?

_____ *B:* No, I can't. But I can use a copy machine.

_____ *B:* Yes, I do. I can use a computer.

_____ *B:* A job as an office assistant.

3 **WRITE** answers to the questions. Then write your own question.

1. What kind of job are you looking for? _____

2. Do you have any skills? _____

3. Can you drive a bus? _____

4. Can you use a cash register? _____

5. Can you use power tools? _____

6. Can you _____? _____

4 **TALK** about your answers with a partner.

Culture and Communication — *Talk about Your Skills*

1 **LISTEN AND CIRCLE.** Listen to the conversations. Circle the correct words.

Useful Expressions
Ways to be positive
Yes, I can… and…
Yes, I can. I like/love to….
Of course I can.
Yes, I can. I'm very good, too.
No, I can't, but I….
I can't, but I'd like to learn.
I can't, but I learn quickly.

1. *A:* Can you **fix / drive** a truck?

   B: Yes, I can. I love to **fix / drive** trucks.

2. *A:* Can you **use / fix** a computer?

   B: No, I can't, but I learn quickly. And I can **fix / use** other machines.

2 **WRITE.** Complete the conversation. Use the expressions in the box.

I'd like to learn	I like to use	but I can speak	~~Nice to meet you~~

Ms. Chan: Good afternoon. My name is Ms. Chan.

Ken: (1) _____*Nice to meet you*_____, Ms. Chan. I'm Ken Davis.

Ms. Chan: So, what kind of job are you looking for?

Ken: A job as an office assistant.

Ms. Chan: OK. What skills do you have?

Ken: Well, I can use a computer. (2) _____ the computer and other office machines.

Ms. Chan: Great. Tell me, can you speak Spanish?

Ken: No, I can't, (3) _____ French, and

(4) _____ Spanish.

Ms. Chan: OK. Please fill out this application.

Ken: Thank you.

Lesson 4

1 MATCH the people with the activities they did yesterday.

__e__	1. The housekeeper	**a.**	worked in the restaurant.
_____	2. The painters	**b.**	studied in the library.
_____	3. The sales clerk	**c.**	measured the cabinets.
_____	4. The students	**d.**	prepared the dinners.
_____	5. The cooks	**e.**	vacuumed the carpets.
_____	6. The servers	**f.**	counted the money.
_____	7. The mechanic	**g.**	painted the house.
_____	8. The carpenter	**h.**	fixed the car.

2 WRITE. Complete the sentences. Use the past tense of the verb.

1. Yesterday I _____ _visited_ _____ (visit) my sister.

2. We _____ (clean) the house.

3. After lunch, I _____ (study) for two hours.

4. My sister _____ (help) our father in the restaurant.

5. They _____ (prepare) some food in the kitchen.

6. Some customers _____ (arrive) at the restaurant at 5:30.

7. They _____ (order) dinner.

8. We _____ (close) the restaurant at 9:00.

3 WRITE. Sara and I didn't do the same things last week. Complete the sentences with the negative forms.

1. Last week, I painted the house. Sara ___didn't paint___ her house.

2. I worked 35 hours. Sara _____ 35 hours.

3. I helped many customers. Sara _____ any customers.

4. I washed my clothes. Sara _____ her clothes.

5. I borrowed a book from the library. Sara _____ any books.

6. I used the computer a lot. Sara _____ the computer at all.

7. I studied Tuesday night. Sara _____ .

8. I ordered some clothes. Sara _____ any clothes.

Lesson 5

1 **WRITE.** Complete the story. Use the past tense of the verbs in parentheses.

Yesterday was not a good day for Al. First, he (1) _____went_____ (go) to the post office.

He (2) _____ (receive) a package from his aunt. On the way home, he dropped the

package. He (3) _____ (break) the beautiful vase. Al was very sad when he

(4) _____ (arrive) at home and (5) _____ (open) the package. Next,

some friends (6) _____ (come) to visit Al. They (7) _____ (make) some

sandwiches for a picnic. They (8) _____ (go) to the park. Everything was fine until it

(9) _____ (start) to rain. It (10) _____ (rain) the whole afternoon, so Al

and his friends (11) _____ (go) home and (12) _____ (watch) a movie.

2 **WHAT ABOUT YOU?** Write sentences using the past tense. Talk about the activities you did or didn't do last week.

1. (make a pie)   _____I made a pie._____ or _____I didn't make a pie._____

2. (receive a package)   _____

3. (go to a restaurant) _____

4. (come to school late) _____

5. (go to the bank)   _____

6. (break a window)   _____

3 **MATH** Read the pay stub and the sentences. Circle *yes* or *no*.

EMPLOYEE NAME		PERIOD BEGINNING	03/21/08
Fatimah Thomas		PERIOD ENDING	03/28/08

SALARY	HOURS	CURRENT $	YEAR TO DATE $
$11.00/Hour	35	$385.00	$4,620.00

Vacation leave balance ON 3/28	Vacation leave used
3 days (21 hours)	2

1. Last week, Fatimah worked 38 hours.   yes   **no**

2. She made $11.00 an hour.   yes   no

3. She received a check for $4,620.   yes   no

4. She used 3 days of vacation leave.   yes   no

5. From 1/1 to 3/21, she received $4,620.   yes   no

Family Connection — *Jobs*

1 **CIRCLE AND WRITE.** Look at the ads. Circle the skills. Then write the occupations.

receptionist	~~carpenter~~	painter	electrician

A: _Carpenter_

Requirements: Use power tools, make door and window frames.

FT position, M–F, 8–4.

Call Jim: 555-1245.

B: _____

Requirements: Use office equipment including computer, fax, copier.

PT position 9 a.m.– 1 p.m. M–F. Small but friendly office.

Call: 555-6767.

C: _____

Must drive a truck. No experience necessary. Will train to paint interior and exterior of houses and apt. bldgs.

Temporary (summer) only. 555-9200.

D. _____

helper wanted.

To fix wires, lights, and fuse boxes; install switches and outlets.

License preferred. FT, good benefits and salary package.

Contact: Will's Electrical Co., 585 Western Avenue, Waltham, or call 555-3880.

2 **WRITE.** Write the answers to the questions.

1. What days do you work in Job A? _Monday, Tuesday, Wednesday, Thursday, Friday_

2. What time do you work in Job A? _____

3. Do you work at night or in the morning in Job B? _____

4. How many hours a week do you work in Job B? _____

5. What season do you work in Job C? _____

6. Is Job D full-time or part-time? _____

3 **READ AND WRITE.** Read about the people. Choose a job. Write the letter of the job from Activity 1.

_____ 1. Sam is a student. He doesn't go to school in the summer. He wants a job. He can drive, but he doesn't have other skills. Which job can Sam do?

_____ 2. Leah likes to build things. She can use power tools. She wants a full-time job. Which job can Leah do?

_____ 3. Herman can work full time. He can fix wires and lights. Which job can he do?

_____ 4. Patti can't work in the afternoon. She can use a computer and answer phones. Which job can she do?

4 **WHAT ABOUT YOU?** What skills do you have? What do you like? Complete the form. Check the skills you have and the things you like. Write your own question. Then write about the jobs you can do.

Can you...	Yes, I can.	No, I can't.	Do you like...	Yes, I do.	No, I don't.
...drive a car?	☐	☐	...cars?	☐	☐
...use a computer?	☐	☐	...computers?	☐	☐
...use power tools?	☐	☐	...to help people?	☐	☐
...prepare food?	☐	☐	...to work alone?	☐	☐
...use a cash register?	☐	☐	...to work outside?	☐	☐
...fix machines?	☐	☐	...to make things?	☐	☐
...	☐	☐	...	☐	☐
What jobs can you do?					

I can be a/an _____

or a/an _____ .

5 **REAL-LIFE LESSON.** Ask a family member about a job. Write a list of skills for that job.

Job	Skills
	_____
	_____
	_____
	_____
	_____
	_____
	_____
	_____

Community Connection — *Apply for a Job*

1 READ AND WRITE. Read and complete the conversation. Use the phrases in the box.

an ad	Did you study	fill out this application
I can fix	~~I'd like to apply for~~	What skills

A: Good afternoon. My name's Stan Sova. (1) *I'd like to apply for* the electrician job.

B: Nice to meet you. I'm Will. Tell me, how did you find out about the job?

A: You have (2) _____ for it in the newspaper.

B: Great. (3) _____ do you have?

A: (4) _____ electrical problems and fix wires in houses.

B: (5) _____ electrical engineering or do you have a license as an electrician?

A: I studied electrical engineering.

B: OK. Then, can you (6) _____ ?

A: Sure. Thank you.

2 WRITE the answers to the questions.

1. What kind of job does Stan want? *He wants a job as an electrician.* _____

2. Where did he see the ad for the job? _____

3. Does Stan have any skills for this job? _____

4. What skills does he have? _____

5. What did Stan study? _____

6. What does Will give Stan to fill out? _____

3 MATCH the questions and the answers.

_d_ 1. What skills do you have?   a. Yes. And I can also drive a forklift.

___ 2. How did you find out about the job?   b. No, but I worked in a restaurant for four years.

___ 3. Did you study?   c. Sure. Thank you very much.

___ 4. Do you have a license as a chef?   d. I can use a computer and a copier.

___ 5. Can you drive a truck?   e. Yes. I studied business for two years.

___ 6. Can you fill out an application?   f. You have an ad for it in the newspaper.

4 WRITE. Complete the conversation. Use your name and information. Use the expressions in the box.

A: Good afternoon. My name's _____ .
_____ the _____ job.

B: Nice to meet you. I'm Will. Tell me, how did you find out about the job?

A: _____ .

B: Great. What skills do you have?

A: _____ .

B: _____ or do you have a license as a/an _____ ?

A: I studied _____ .

B: OK. Then, can you fill out this application?

A: _____ .

5 WRITE. Complete the application. Use your information.

Name: _____
Telephone #: _____

Position wanted: _____

Address: _____
_____

Days and hours available: _____
_____

Skills:

WORK EXPERIENCE

Dates: _____
Employer: _____
Present or last position: _____
Responsibilities: _____

How did you find out about the job? _____ Signature: _____

6 REAL-LIFE LESSON. Find three want ads or signs for jobs. What information is in the ads or signs?

Name of job	PT/FT	Skills or requirements	Who do you call or talk to?
1.			
2.			
3.			

Career Connection — *Self-Assessment Forms*

1 **READ AND CIRCLE.** Isabel answered questions about her work. Read her self-assessment. Then circle the things she can improve.

Monthly Self-Assessment	
Month: *September*	**Position:** *Office assistant*

Think about your work this week. What did you do? How well did you work?
+ = great work; always
✓ = good work; sometimes
— = can improve
N/A = not applicable (not part of your work)

Did you...

✓	(arrive on time?)
+	clean your tools and work area?
+	answer phones politely?
N/A	help customers politely?
—	check your reports for spelling?
✓	complete your work on time?
—	learn something new?
✓	fix any errors or mistakes?
✓	help your co-workers?
✓	report any problems to your supervisor?

What can you do to improve your work?
I can use "Spell Check" on the computer to help my spelling.
I can ask co-workers to check my spelling before I give the reports to the supervisor.
I can look online and on the company bulletin board to find job training classes.
I can ask my co-workers about job training classes.

2 **WRITE.** Answer the questions about Isabel's form.

1. Does Isabel always arrive on time? _____

2. How many things did Isabel check "+"? _____

3. What things does Isabel do very well? _____

4. How many things did Isabel check "—"? _____

5. What does Isabel need to improve? _____

6. What ideas does Isabel have to improve her work? _____

3 **WHAT ABOUT YOU?** Think about a job you did or how you studied English last month. What did you do? Did you do a good job? What can you improve? Complete the chart about you.

What I did...	What I can improve...
I arrived on time.	I can complete my work on time.

🖥 **Technology Connection:** How to Use a Computer Spell Check

4 **PRACTICE** the Spell Check program on the computer screen. Write the letter to show the part of the screen.

A

Spelling and Grammar

Not in dictionary

| wourd _____ **E** | **Ignore** |

Suggestions   **B**   **Change**

word	
wood ——————— **D**	**Add**
would **C**	**Cancel**

_A_ **1.** Open "Spell Check."

        The program starts at the beginning and checks the spelling of all the words.

_____ **2.** It stops when a word is wrong.

_____ **3.** The program gives you a suggestion (another word or another spelling for the word).

_____ **4.** Click on "Change" to correct the word.

_____ **5.** Click on "Cancel" when you are finished checking.

Practice Test

WCD, 37

LISTENING: Listen to the conversations. Then choose the correct answer for each sentence.

1.
   A. No, I can't, but I'd like to learn.
   B. Yes, I can use power tools.
   C. A construction worker.
   D. No, I didn't.

2.
   A. I was a salesclerk.
   B. I can cook Chinese food.
   C. They are servers.
   D. No, I can't, but I can use a cash register.

3. What job did he have?
   A. a teacher
   B. a plumber
   C. an electrician
   D. a receptionist

4. What did he do?
   A. He studied wires.
   B. He made wires.
   C. He made problems.
   D. He fixed wires.

5. He worked with _____.
   A. his brother
   B. his father
   C. a friend
   D. a teacher

GRAMMAR AND VOCABULARY: Choose the correct word to complete each sentence.

6. Jim's a mechanic. He can _____ .
   A. use a cash register
   B. prepare food
   C. fix cars
   D. fix water pipes

7. A _____ can make cabinets.
   A. plumber
   B. dentist
   C. server
   D. carpenter

8. Can Davinder use a computer?
   A. Yes, we can.
   B. Yes, he can.
   C. Yes, I can.
   D. Yes, they can.

9. Can you speak Korean?
   A. No, they can't.
   B. No, you can't.
   C. No, I can't.
   D. No, she can't.

10. My brother _____ our house last week.
   A. painted
   B. painter
   C. paint
   D. paints

11. We _____ study last night.
   A. didn't
   B. don't
   C. can't
   D. aren't

12. Did George go to work yesterday?
    Yes, he _____ to work.
    A. go
    B. going
    C. went
    D. goes

13. Did you make those cabinets?
    Yes, I _____ them last year.
    A. made
    B. make
    C. making
    D. do

14. Eva didn't _____ on time yesterday.
    A. arrived
    B. arrive
    C. arrives
    D. arriving

15. Li _____ home at 8:00 last night.
    A. come
    B. comes
    C. can
    D. came

READING: Read the ad. Then choose the correct answer.

Receptionist For Busy Office.

Do you like to answer phones?
Can you use a computer and a
fax machine?

We need you! M, T, TH. 9–5.
Call Ms. Jones: 555-4321.

16. This is a _____.
    A. job application
    B. office directory
    C. job ad
    D. school course

17. What skill does a receptionist have?
    A receptionist can _____.
    A. drive a truck
    B. answer phones
    C. order food
    D. order supplies

18. The receptionist doesn't _____.
    A. use a computer
    B. use power tools
    C. use a fax machine
    D. answer phones

19. This job is _____ days a week.
    A. 3
    B. 5
    C. 7
    D. 4

20. How many hours a day is the job? _____
    A. 9 hours a day
    B. 8 hours a day
    C. 3 hours a day
    D. 5 hours a day

UNIT 10 Taking a Trip

Lesson 1

1 LOOK AND WRITE. Look at the picture. Write the letter of the places.

_H_ **1.** bus   ____ **4.** airport   ____ **7.** baggage claim

____ **2.** airplane   ____ **5.** train station   ____ **8.** bus stop

____ **3.** train   ____ **6.** ticket counter   ____ **9.** platform

2 WRITE. Complete the (+) sentences with *was* or *were*. Complete the (–) sentences with *wasn't* or *weren't*.

1. (–) Last week, we ____*weren't*____ at school.

2. (+) We _____ at the train station.

3. (+) I _____ at the ticket counter.

4. (–) The tickets for the train _____ expensive.

5. (+) There _____ many people waiting for the train.

6. (+) Jana and Elena _____ on the platform waiting for the train.

7. (–) The train _____ on time.

8. (–) So, we _____ happy.

9. (–) You _____ with us.

10. (+) You _____ at the airport.

Lesson 2

1 **WRITE.** The class starts at 7:30. Complete the sentences with *was/were* and *early, on time,* or *late*.

1. I arrived at 7:23. I _____was early_____.

2. Pete arrived at 7:35. He _____.

3. The teacher arrived at 7:15. She _____.

4. Tom and Maya arrived at 7:30. They _____.

5. You arrived at 7:45. You _____.

6. Lilia arrived at 7:30. She _____.

2 **READ AND WRITE.** Read the sentences. Then write the words in the puzzle.

1. Randy takes his bag from the baggage _c_ _l_ [a] _i_ _m_ .

2. It's not quiet. It's ___ ___ [ ] ___ _y_ .

3. There are too many people there. It's very ___ [ ] ___ _w_ ___ ___ _d_ .

4. Usually Randy waits for the train on the [ ] _l_ ___ ___ _f_ ___ ___ ___ .

5. Sometimes he waits for the bus at the bus ___ ___ [ ] _p_ .

6. Randy wasn't late today. He was ___ _a_ [ ] ___ ___ .

7. He's going on vacation. He was at the ticket _c_ ___ ___ _u_ ___ [ ] ___ ___ to buy his ticket.

LOOK at the letters in the boxes. Where is Randy? He's at the ___ ___ ___ ___ ___ ___ ___ .

3 **WHAT ABOUT YOU?** Complete the sentences with a word in the box or your own idea.

early	~~on time~~	late	bus	train	airplane	quiet	crowded	noisy

1. I was _____on time_____ for class today.

2. I was _____ for work yesterday.

3. I was on a/an _____ last week.

4. The bus was _____ today.

5. I was on a/an _____ last year.

6. I wasn't on a/an _____ yesterday.

7. The _____ was late this morning.

Lesson 3

1 **LISTEN AND CHECK** the meaning.

1. ☐ There's a problem.   ☑ I'm upset.

2. ☐ There's a problem.   ☐ I'm upset.

3. ☐ There's a problem.   ☐ I'm upset.

4. ☐ Yes   ☐ No

5. ☐ Yes   ☐ No

6. ☐ Yes   ☐ No

2 **WRITE.** Complete the conversation. Use the words in the box.

| important customer | call next time | I'm late | the bus | I'm so sorry | You missed |

A: I'm sorry (1) _____ *I'm late* _____. I missed

(2) _____.

B: I see. (3) _____ an (4) _____.

A: Oh, no. (5) _____.

B: Well, please (6) _____.

3 **MATCH** the questions and answers.

__c__ 1. How much is the fare?

_____ 2. How long is the train ride?

_____ 3. When does the train leave?

_____ 4. When does the train arrive?

_____ 5. Are there other trains?

_____ 6. When do they leave?

_____ 7. Is the train usually on time?

_____ 8. Is there sometimes a problem with the train?

a. Yes, there are.

b. It arrives at 2:00 P.M.

c. It's $35.00.

d. At 11:30 A.M. and 3:30 P.M.

e. Yes, it is.

f. It leaves at 10:00 A.M.

g. Yes, there is. Sometimes the train is too crowded.

h. It's four hours.

Culture and Communication — *Call To Say You're Late*

1 **LISTEN AND WRITE.** Listen to the conversations. Write the response.

A: <u>I'm sorry.</u> The bus was 30 minutes late! I'm late for work.

B: _____

_____

_____

_____

A: Oops! Sorry. I missed the bus.

B: _____

_____

_____

_____

a. Well, please call next time.

b. No problem.

2 **WRITE.** Complete the conversation. Use the phrases in the box or your own ideas.

30 minutes late	I'm really sorry	late for work
No problem	take your phone calls	What time

Kati: Hi. Ernesto. This is Kati. (1) _____ *I'm really sorry* _____.

The bus was (2) _____ I So, I'm

(3) _____.

Ernesto: OK. (4) _____ are you arriving?

Kati: Probably 9:30.

Ernesto: (5) _____. I can

(6) _____.

Useful Expressions

Ways to apologize
I'm sorry.
I'm so sorry.
I'm really sorry.
I had a problem.
I didn't expect this.

3 **READ AND CHECK.** It's important to be on time. Sometimes it's very important to call. Read the situations. Check the situations that you need to call. You are …

1. ☑ 15 minutes late for work.

2. ☐ 2 minutes late for a class.

3. ☐ 1 hour late for a doctor's appointment.

4. ☐ 15 minutes late for a party.

5. ☐ 5 minutes late for a meeting with your boss.

Lesson 4

1 **WRITE** the names of the places.

amusement park	beach	museum	movie	~~mountains~~	lake

1. mountains

2. _____

3. _____

4. _____

5. _____

6. _____

2 **READ AND WRITE.** Read about the people. Where did they go on vacation? Use the words from Activity 1.

1. Raul likes to swim and relax. He _____ *went to the beach* _____.

2. Manolo likes to take long walks. He _____.

3. Marika and Josh like to look at pictures and art. They

   _____.

4. Taylor likes to ride roller coasters. She also likes to be with lots of people and have fun. She

   _____.

5. Jeff and Danielle like boats and fishing. They _____.

6. Hana likes to watch movies and films. She _____.

3 **MATCH** the opposites. Write the letter.

___c___ **1.** slow   **a.** interesting

_____ **2.** clean   **b.** hot

_____ **3.** boring   **c.** fast

_____ **4.** relaxing   **d.** dirty

_____ **5.** cold   **e.** stressful

4 **WRITE.** Complete the questions and answers. Use *was/were* or *wasn't/weren't*.

1. ____Was____ the hotel clean?   Yes, it ____was____.

2. _____ the roads to the mountains dangerous?   No, they _____.

3. _____ the weather hot?   Yes, it _____.

4. _____ the traffic slow?   No, it _____.

5. _____ the lake dirty?   No, it _____.

6. _____ the amusement park rides scary?   Yes, they _____.

7. _____ you on time for the train?   No, I _____.

8. _____ you and Ines late?   No, we _____.

5 **MATH.** Look at the bus schedule. Complete the missing information.

Bus	Departs Boston	Arrives New York	How long?
A	6:15 A.M.	10:45 A.M.	4:30
B	7:25 A.M.	12:10 P.M.	_____
C	9:50 A.M.	2:20 P.M.	_____
D	11:30 A.M.	_____ P.M.	4:35
E	2:45 P.M.	_____ P.M.	4:30
F	6:15 P.M.	10:30 P.M.	_____

6 **WRITE** answers to the questions. Use the bus schedule in Activity 5.

1. Michelle went to New York for a meeting. The meeting was at 12:00 P.M. Which bus did she take?
   ___Bus A___

2. Greg went to New York to watch a baseball game. The game started at 7:00 P.M. Which bus did he take? _____

3. Nick and Andy went to meet some friends at a restaurant at 8:00 P.M. Which bus did they take? _____

4. Elena went for a job interview. Her interview was at 4:00 P.M. Which bus did she take? _____

5. Raul ate breakfast with his cousin at 8:00 A.M. They ate at Raul's hotel. Which bus did Raul take?
   _____

6. Helen went to the art museum. She went in the morning and stayed all day. Which bus did she take?
   _____

Family Connection—*Pay the Fare*

1 READ AND WRITE. Read the definitions. Write the words under the illustrations.

> ### How to Pay the Fare
>
> **exact change:** coins (quarters, dimes, nickels) that is the correct amount of money
> **tokens:** pieces of metal that you use instead of money
> **pass:** a card from the bus or transportation company
> **ticket:** a piece of paper to show that you paid the fare

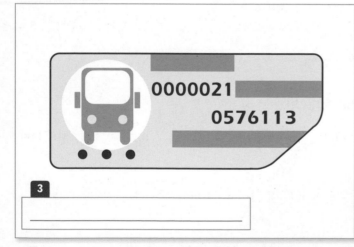

1

_____pass_____

2

_____

3

_____

4

_____

2 READ AND WRITE. Complete the sentences. Use the words in Activity 1.

1. Nancy uses three quarters to pay the fare. She is using _____.

2. Sukwinder buys a _____ every month to ride the bus.

3. Oscar uses two _____ every day to ride the subway to and from work.

4. Cheng doesn't often ride the bus. He buys a _____ to ride the bus to the park.

3 READ AND WRITE. Complete the conversations. Use the words in the box.

it doesn't	the fare	it's an express	Bus 57
this bus stop	local bus	exact change	~~this bus go~~

Tran: Excuse me. Does (1) _____this bus go_____ to the mall?

Bus driver: No, (2) _____. You want (3) _____.

Tran: 56?

Bus driver: No, 57. It's over there.

Tran: Thanks.

Celia: Does (4) _____ at Park Square?

Bus driver: No, (5) _____ to Centerville. There aren't other stops.

Celia: Which bus do I need?

Bus driver: You want the (6) _____, Bus 34. It stops at Park Square.

Celia: How much is (7) _____?

Bus driver: $1.25.

Celia: Can I use cash?

Bus driver: Yes, but you need (8) _____.

Celia: Thank you.

4 CIRCLE yes or no.

1. Tran gets on the bus at Park Square.　　　　yes　　(no)

2. The bus driver is in Bus 57.　　　　yes　　no

3. Tran wants Bus 57.　　　　yes　　no

4. Celia is going to Centerville.　　　　yes　　no

5. The express bus stops at Park Square.　　　　yes　　no

6. The local bus costs $1.25.　　　　yes　　no

5 REAL-LIFE LESSON. How do your friends and family get to work and school? Ask the questions and write their answers.

1. Do you take a bus, subway, or train? _____

2. Do you use exact change, tokens, or a pass? _____

3. Where do you get on and off? _____

Community Connection — *Subway Map*

1 **LOOK AND CIRCLE.** Look at the map of three subway lines. Circle the correct words.

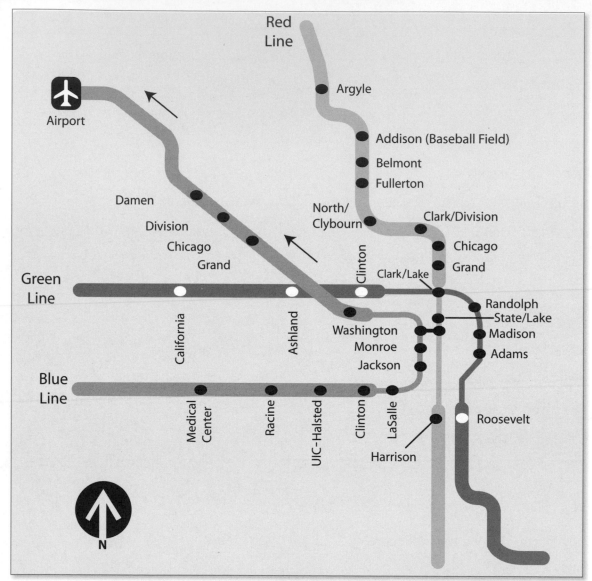

1. Julia gets on the subway at Belmont. She gets off at Harrison. She takes the **green** / **red** line.

2. Luis gets on the subway at Ashland and gets off at Madison. He takes the **red** / **green** line.

3. Julia goes to the airport. She takes the **green** / **blue** line.

4. Julia gets on at Belmont. To get to the airport, she changes subway lines at the subway stop at **Clark/Lake** / **Washington**.

5. Luis goes to a baseball game at Baseball Field (Addison). He takes the **blue** / **red** line.

6. Luis gets on the subway at Ashland. To get to the baseball game, he changes subway lines at **Clark/Lake** / **State/Lake**.

2 READ AND WRITE. Read and complete the conversation. Use the map in Activity 1 and the words in the box.

the subway	the red line	What time	the airport
on time	the blue line	~~Where~~	the last stop

Julia: Hi, Ema. (1) _____ *Where* _____ are you going?

Ema: To Colorado on vacation. Do you know how to get to the airport on

(2) _____?

Julia: Sure. We're at Belmont. So take (3) _____ downtown.

Change at Washington to (4) _____.

Ema: OK. Which way?

Julia: The airport is (5) _____. So get on the train to

(6) _____.

Ema: Thanks. I hope I get there (7) _____.

Julia: (8) _____ does your plane leave?

Ema: 7:30.

Julia: It's 5:30 now. So you can get there on time. Have a good trip!

Ema: Thanks again. I'll send you a postcard!

3 WRITE answers to the questions about the conversation.

1. Where is Ema going? _____ *She's going to Colorado.* _____

2. Is the airport on the red line or the blue line? _____

3. Where does Ema change to the blue line? _____

4. Does Ema's plane leave at 7:30 or at 5:30? _____

4 WRITE. Look at the subway map in Activity 1. Sergei is going from Harrison to Medical Center. Complete the directions for him.

1. Get on at _____ *Ashland* _____.

2. Take the _____ downtown.

3. Change at _____ and take the _____.

4. Get off at _____.

Career Connection — *Online Traffic Reports*

1 READ. Isabel is talking to her boss, Laura. Laura is in an airport in another city. She is renting a car and driving from the airport to a meeting. Isabel checks the traffic report. There's a problem on the highway. Match the words with the definitions.

__c__ **1.** to avoid   **a.** an explanation or presentation of information

_____ **2.** traffic   **b.** a different way to get to a place

_____ **3.** highway   **c.** to stay away from

_____ **4.** report   **d.** a large main road

_____ **5.** alternate route   **e.** cars and trucks on the road

2 READ AND WRITE. Read Isabel's conversation with Laura. Write the words from Activity 1 in the conversation.

> *Isabel:* Your car is ready at the airport when you arrive in Atlanta.
>
> *Laura:* Great! Tell me, is there a lot of (1) _____*traffic*_____ on the roads around the city?
>
> *Isabel:* Just a minute. Let me check the local (2). Oh, no. There's a problem on the (3) _____ near the airport.
>
> *Laura:* That is a problem. Can you check if there is an (4) _____? I want to get to the meeting on time.
>
> *Isabel:* Sure. Let me check an online map. Yes, you can go on Route 7 to Route 5
>
> (5) _____ the problem.

3 LOOK AND WRITE. Look at the road signs. Write the letter of the sign next to the meaning.

_D_ **1.** rocks on the road

_____ **2.** water on the road

_____ **3.** There's a problem with the road. You can't drive on it.

_____ **4.** There's a problem on the road. You need to take another road.

_____ **5.** workers on the road

_____ **6.** Is there an emergency? Stay here.

_____ **7.** Is there a bad storm? Leave on this road.

_____ **8.** landslide (mud, rocks, and dirt) or avalanche (snow) on the road

---

Technology Connection: Use an Online Map

4 **LOOK AND CIRCLE.** Isabel uses an online map to find a new route for Laura. Read the instructions. Circle the correct words.

1. (Open)/ **Close** the online map.

2. Click on "**Search the map**" / "**Get directions**."

3. Enter the starting **telephone number** / **address**.

4. **Enter** / **Read** the end address.

5. **Check** / **Write** the box "Avoid highways."

6. Click "**Find**" / "**Close**."

7. Look at the **calendar** / **map** and directions.

---

5 **REAL-LIFE LESSON.** Ask friends, family members, or coworkers which websites have local traffic reports for your city or town. Then ask which online maps they use.

Local traffic reports are at...	Online maps are at...
sigalert.com	maps.google.com

Unit 10 Test

LISTENING: Listen to the conversations. Then choose the correct answer for each sentence.

1.
   A. I went to the mountains for vacation.
   B. Oh, no. I'm so sorry.
   C. It was boring.
   D. The bus was late this morning.

2.
   A. The traffic was really bad.
   B. Oh, no. I'm so sorry.
   C. Was it fun?
   D. Please call next time.

3. Where did Margot go on vacation?
   A. to the beach
   B. to the movies
   C. to the mountains
   D. to the lake

4. Was it fun?
   A. No, it was too noisy.
   B. No, it was boring.
   C. Yes, it was.
   D. Yes, but it was dirty.

5. How was the hotel?
   A. It was dirty and crowded.
   B. It was cold and noisy.
   C. It was clean and crowded.
   D. It was empty and quiet.

GRAMMAR AND VOCABULARY: Choose the correct word to complete each sentence.

6. Yesterday I _____ in a boat at the lake.
   A. was
   B. am
   C. were
   D. do

7. Celia and Karen _____ in school last week.
   A. aren't
   B. wasn't
   C. isn't
   D. weren't

8. _____ Ines on time for work?
   A. Was
   B. Are
   C. Do
   D. Were

9. Were you sick yesterday? No, I _____.
   A. weren't
   B. am not
   C. wasn't
   D. aren't

10. My trip was not boring. It was very _____.
   A. interesting
   B. relaxing
   C. stressful
   D. slow

11. There were many people on the bus.
    It was _____.
   A. quiet
   B. early
   C. late
   D. crowded

12. Tom is at the platform. He's waiting for the _____.
    A. bus
    B. train
    C. airplane
    D. taxi

13. I need to get my bag at the _____.
    A. ticket counter
    B. airport
    C. platform
    D. baggage claim

14. How much is the fare?
    A. It's $7.25.
    B. It's ten minutes late.
    C. At 12:00.
    D. It's one hour.

15. When does the train arrive?
    A. Two hours.
    B. At 2:30.
    C. It's late.
    D. It's on time.

READING: Read the schedule. Then choose the correct answer.

Bus	Departs Miami	Arrives Orlando	Fare	How long?
A	4:45 A.M.	10:30 A.M.	$41.25	5:45
B	10:20 A.M.	5:05 P.M.	$41.25	6:45
C	1:20 P.M.	7:20 P.M.	$41.25	6:00
D	7:15 P.M.	12:35 P.M.	$41.25	5:20

16. This is a _____ schedule.
    A. train
    B. airplane
    C. bus
    D. work

17. Pam leaves Miami at 10:20. What time does she get to Orlando?
    A. 5:05
    B. 6:45
    C. 10:30
    D. 4:25

18. Tim arrives in Orlando at 7:20 in the evening. What time did he leave Miami?
    A. 4:45
    B. 6:00
    C. 1:20
    D. 5:05

19. How much is the fare?
    A. $5.20
    B. $7.15
    C. $14.25
    D. $41.25

20. Eva was on the bus for 6 hours and 45 minutes. Which bus did she take?
    A. Bus A
    B. Bus B
    C. Bus C
    D. Bus D

Lesson 1

1 MATCH. Look at the picture. Match the people with the problems.

Sergei

Erin

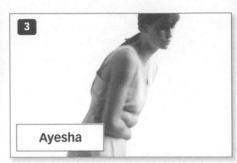
Ayesha

Rinaldo

Esmerelda's son

Jacinta

___d___ **1.** Sergei has

_____ **2.** Erin has

_____ **3.** Ayesha has

_____ **4.** Rinaldo has

_____ **5.** Esmerelda's son has

_____ **6.** Jacinta has

a. a fever.

b. a toothache.

c. a cough.

d. a headache.

e. a sore throat.

f. a stomachache.

2 WRITE. Complete the sentences. Use *has/have* or *doesn't have/don't have*.

1. Irina and Ana _____*have*_____ colds.

2. John isn't OK. He _____ a backache.

3. I don't feel OK. I _____ a runny nose.

4. Marc's children are sick. They _____ stomachaches.

5. We aren't sick. We _____ sore throats.

6. Sopal is OK. He _____ the flu.

7. Rachel feels OK. She _____ an earache.

8. You're OK. You _____ a fever.

Lesson 2

1 **WRITE** the parts of the body. Use the words from the box. Then complete the sentences. Use *hurt* or *hurts* and a word from the box.

nose	stomach	feet	back	~~head~~	hands	neck	ear

1. Are you OK?   No, my _____head hurts_____ .

2. Is Allen OK?   No, his _____ .

3. Is Nate OK?   No, his _____ .

4. Are you OK?   No, my _____ .

5. Is Paula OK?   No, her _____ .

6. Are you and Greg OK? No, our _____ .

7. Are Mike and Sam OK? No, their _____ .

8. Is your sister OK?   No, her _____ .

2 **WRITE.** Complete the sentences. Use the words in the box.

flu	head	feet	nose	stomach	cold
back	fever	throat	hands	~~ears~~	toothache

1. When the office is noisy, _____my ears hurt_____ .

2. When Dan runs, _____ .

3. When Anna reads, _____ .

4. When my father eats Thai food, _____ .

5. When Hiro carries heavy machines, _____ .

6. When I talk a lot, _____ .

7. When I don't brush my teeth, I get a _____ .

8. When I have the _____ , I get a _____ .

9. When I use the computer a lot, my _____ hurt.

10. When I have a _____ , I have a runny _____ .

Lesson 3

1 LISTEN. the questions and answers.

_f_ **1.** What's wrong?   **a.** Yes, it is.

____ **2.** How do you feel?   **b.** No, I'm sick.

____ **3.** Do you have a cold?   **c.** No, it doesn't.

____ **4.** Are you OK?   **d.** My stomach hurts.

____ **5.** Does your head hurt? **e.** Yes, I do.

____ **6.** Is your throat sore? **f.** I feel terrible.

2 WRITE. Complete the conversation. Use the words in the box.

come to work	That's too bad	a lot of people	My stomach
a fever	~~I'm sick~~	get well soon	What's wrong

A: Hello?

B: Hi. This is Kara.

A: Hi, Kara. You sound terrible. Are you OK?

B: No, (1) ____ *I'm sick* ____ . I can't (2) _____ today.

A: I'm sorry. (3) _____ ?

B: (4) _____ hurts and I have (5) _____ .

A: (6) _____ . There are (7) _____ out sick this week.

B: Really?

A: Yes. Well, (8) _____ .

B: OK. Thanks.

3 LISTEN AND MATCH. Listen to the phone calls. Match the person with the problem.

WCD, 41

_c_ **1.** Kevin   **a.** the flu

____ **2.** Alicia   **b.** a headache and cough

____ **3.** Anh-Li   **c.** a sore throat and a fever

____ **4.** Tung   **d.** an earache and a fever

Culture and Communication—*Talk about How You Feel*

1 **LISTEN.** Read the conversation.

WCD, 42

Monica: Sara, <u>are you all right?</u>

Sara: Hi, Monica. No, not really.

Monica: <u>What's the problem?</u>

Sara: I have a runny nose and a fever. Do you think I have the flu?

Monica: Maybe. Talk to the boss. You should leave early and go home to rest.

Sara: That's a good idea.

Monica: I hope you feel better.

Sara: Thanks. Me, too.

2 **CIRCLE** *yes* or *no*.

1. Sara feels terrible. (yes) no
2. Monica has a problem. yes no
3. Monica thinks Sara has a cold. yes no
4. Monica wants to go home early. yes no
5. Sara should go home and rest. yes no
6. Sara can talk to the boss. yes no

Useful Expressions
Ways to ask how someone feels
How are you?
Do you feel all right?/OK?
Are you all right/OK?
What's wrong?
What's the matter?
What's the problem?

3 **WHAT ABOUT YOU?** Read the situations. Check what you can do. More than one answer is possible.

When I have....,	go to work/ school.	stay home.	go to the doctor or clinic.	go to the hospital.
a headache, I...	✓			
a toothache, I...				
a stomachache and a fever, I...				
a fever, I...				
an earache and a fever, I...				
a cold, I...				

Lesson 4

1 **MATCH** the parts of the sentences.

   _f_   **1.** The students should   **a.** liquids.

        2. Emily should use a   **b.** a doctor.

        3. You should drink   **c.** ice on her hand.

        4. Ed should put   **d.** prescription for their coughs.

        5. They should get a   **e.** a bandage on his foot.

        6. I should call   **f.** rest.

        7. You should see   **g.** 911.

        8. Ann should put   **h.** heating pad.

2 **WRITE** *should* or *shouldn't* in the sentences.

1. Richard has a backache. He _____*should*_____ use a heating pad.

2. We have colds. We _____ drink juice.

3. You have the flu. You _____ go to work.

4. Lin and Helen have coughs. They _____ call 911.

5. Ivan has a sore throat. He _____ take a throat lozenge.

6. Kara's feet hurt. She _____ rest.

7. Adam has a runny nose. He _____ call 911.

8. Jaqui's knee hurts. She _____ put ice on it. She _____ play tennis.

9. Erik's neck hurts. He _____ go to an amusement park. He _____ get a prescription for a pain reliever.

3 **LISTEN.** Circle *should* or *shouldn't*.

1. You **should** / **shouldn't** put ice on it.

2. Glen **should** / **shouldn't** go to work.

3. They **should** / **shouldn't** put ice on them.

4. Nancy **should** / **shouldn't** see a doctor.

5. He **should** / **shouldn't** use some ear drops.

6. We **should** / **shouldn't** eat hot food.

Lesson 5

1 **READ AND WRITE.** Complete the conversation. Use *should* or *shouldn't*.

Tyler: Ow. My back hurts.

Pam: Really? You (1) _____shouldn't_____ lift those heavy boxes. How much do they weigh?

Tyler: About 80 pounds. Ow!

Pam: Wait. You (2) _____ lift with your back. You can hurt your back. You (3) _____ use your legs to lift.

Tyler: That's better. But my back still hurts.

Pam: Sure. It will be sore for a few days. Do you have a heating pad?

Tyler: Yes, I do.

Pam: Well, you (4) _____ use that for a couple of hours tonight.

Tyler: (5) _____ I take a pain reliever? What do you think?

Pam: You (6) _____ take some tonight—maybe tomorrow. Read the label to see how much you (7) _____ take.

Tyler: That's a good idea.

2 **MATH.** Read the medicine label. Answer the questions.

COLD RELIEF

For relief from cold symptoms (runny nose, cough, and headache).

Directions: Take two pills every 4 hours as needed. Do not take more than 8 in 24 hours.

1. Teresa takes 2 pills at 11:00 A.M. What time should she take COLD RELIEF again? _____3:00 P.M._____

2. Seydor takes 2 pills at 8:00 A.M., 2 more at 12:00 P.M., and 2 more at 4:00 P.M. He still feels terrible at 8 P.M. Should he take 2 more pills? _____

3. Renata takes 2 pills at 6:00 A.M. and 2 more at 12:00 P.M. What time should she take more? _____

4. Ali takes 2 pills at 6:30 A.M., 2 at 10:30 A.M., 2 at 2:30 P.M., and 2 at 6:30 P.M. Should he take 2 more pills at 10:30 P.M.? _____

Family Connection — *Call for a Medical Appointment*

1 **MATCH** the words and their meanings.

__e__ **1.** a rash   **a.** a place where doctors and nurses work

_____ **2.** a fever   **b.** a free time in a schedule

_____ **3.** take your temperature   **c.** a meeting at a specific time and place

_____ **4.** an appointment   **d.** a body temperature that is too hot (higher than 98.6° F)

_____ **5.** an opening   **e.** a red spot or spots on your skin

_____ **6.** a clinic   **f.** use a thermometer to check if you have a fever

2 **READ AND WRITE.** Read and complete the conversation. Use the words in the box.

the doctor	Is that OK?	~~I help you~~	a rash	her birthdate
my daughter	her temperature	daughter's name	an opening	

Clinic: Good afternoon. Williston Health Clinic. How can (1) _____ *I help you* _____?

Mrs. Lang: I'm calling about (2) _____. She has a fever and

                (3) _____. Can (4) _____ see her?

Clinic: OK. What's your (5) _____?

Mrs. Lang: Denise Lang.

Clinic: What's (6) _____?

Mrs. Lang: April 12, 2004.

Clinic: Did you take (7) _____?

Mrs. Lang: Yes, I did. It was 102 degrees.

Clinic: All right. That's high. Let me see. I have (8) _____ this afternoon at

                3:00. (9) _____?

Mrs. Lang: Yes, that's fine. So, the appointment is this afternoon at 3:00.

Clinic: Right. We'll see you then. And please bring your insurance card.

Mrs. Lang: OK. Thank you.

3 **WRITE.** You are calling the clinic for an appointment. Someone in your family is sick. Complete the conversation. Use the conversation above as a model.

Clinic: Good afternoon. Williston Health Clinic.

You: I'm calling about _____. He/She has _____ and _____. Can we get an appointment?

Clinic: OK. What's your _____'s name?

You: _____.

Clinic: What's his/her birthdate?

You: _____

Clinic: Did you take his/her temperature?

You: Yes, I did. It was _____ degrees.

Clinic: All right. That's high. Let me see. The doctor has an opening _____
(day/date) at _____ (time).

You: Yes, that's fine. So, the appointment is _____ (day/date) at _____ (time).

Clinic: Right. We'll see you then. And please bring in your insurance card.

You: Yes. Thank you.

4 **WRITE.** Complete the doctor's appointment card using the information from your conversation in Activity 4.

5 **REAL-LIFE LESSON.** Ask a family member or neighbor about a doctor's appointment. Use these questions or your own.

Williston Health Clinic

_____

Has an appointment on: _____
(day, date)

At: _____ A.M. / P.M.
(time)

With: _Dr. Jones_____

Please call (414) 555-2020 if you need to cancel your appointment

---

1. Do you call to get an appointment or do you go to the office? _____

2. Do you usually get an appointment for that day? _____

3. How often do you go to the doctor? _____

4. When do you usually go to the doctor? (Do you go when you're sick? Do you go for check-ups every year?) _____

5. Does the clinic call to remind you of appointments? _____

6. Do you get cards with the date and time of the appointment? _____

Community Connection—*Injuries*

1 **MATCH** the pictures with the injuries.

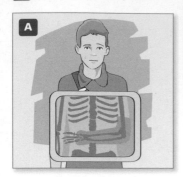 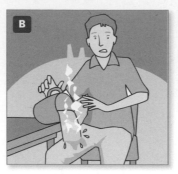  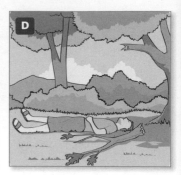

___c___ **1.** His hand is bleeding.

_____ **2.** He has a burn on his leg.

_____ **3.** He's unconscious.

_____ **4.** He has a broken arm.

2 **WRITE.** Unscramble the words. Write sentences about how the injuries in Activity 1 happened.

1. hand / his / cut / Tom / a / knife / with ___Tom cut his hand with a knife___ .

2. water / hot / on / A / pot / of / fell / leg / his _____ .

3. head / Raul / his / hit _____ .

4. her / fell / Jill / bicycle / off _____ .

3 **READ AND CIRCLE** the correct words.

➕ FIRST AID AND EMERGENCIES ➕

A: For Burns (first or second degree)

1. First, you **should** / **shouldn't** put cool water over the burn (15–30 minutes).
2. Next, **clean / take** the burn with soap and water.
3. If blisters are open, you **should put / should clean** a dry bandage over the area.
4. You **can use / can't go** an antibiotic ointment on the burn.
5. You **can move / can't use** an antibiotic ointment on open blisters.
6. **Take / Don't take** a pain reliever as needed.

B: For a Broken Bone

1. Go to the **emergency room / drugstore** for x-rays and treatment. Then, . . .

2. **Use / Don't use** the arm or leg. Use a sling or crutches.

3. You **should / shouldn't** put ice on it to reduce any pain and swelling.

4. Use a bandage so you **move / don't move** the arm or leg.

5. You **should / shouldn't** use a pain reliever as needed.

4 **WRITE.** Make a list of things you need for burns and broken bones in a first aid kit. Use Activity 3 for ideas.

For burns, you need . . .	For a broken bone, you need . . .
cool water	ice

5 **REAL-LIFE LESSON.** Ask a family member or neighbor about where he or she gets medical help. Use these questions or your own.

1. Do you go to a clinic or a doctor's office when you are sick? _____

2. Where do you go for an emergency? _____

3. Who is your doctor? _____

4. Who is your dentist? _____

5. Where can you get more information about clinics, doctors, and hospitals?

   _____

6. Does your insurance pay for all or some of the doctor's and hospital's fees?

   _____

7. _____?

   _____

Career Connection—*Read Insurance Forms*

1 READ. Isabel's boss, Laura, had the flu. She went to the doctor. She received this paper from her health insurance company.

Excellent Health Care, Inc.
P.O. Box 744
Centerville, NY 11732

Explanation of Benefits

Laura Markham   3/15/80

Subscriber Name: Laura Markham
Certificate Number: 955-34-3025

Group Name: CMC
Group Number: 03534

Type of Service/Date	Charges	Amount allowed	Benefit Paid	Amount Due from Patient
Laura Markham Williston Health Clinic Amarjit Singh MD				
Lab 2/23/08	$57.00	$29.06	$29.06	$27.94
Pharmacy 2/23/08	$70.20	$49.14	$49.14	$21.06
SUMMARY 3/10/08	$127.20	$78.20	$78.20	$49.00

For Assistance, please call: 8:00 a.m.–4:30 p.m. Monday–Friday **1-800-555-2277**

2 MATCH the questions and answers about Activity 1.

___d___ **1.** Who is the patient?

_____ **2.** Who is the doctor?

_____ **3.** What is the total cost of the lab work?

_____ **4.** What is the total cost of the pharmacy?

_____ **5.** How much of the bills does the insurance company pay?

_____ **6.** How much does Laura pay?

a. Amarjit Singh, MD

b. $78.20

c. $49.00

d. Laura Markham

e. $57.00

f. $70.20

3 CIRCLE the answers about the insurance paper in Activity 1.

1. Laura went to the clinic on March 15, 1980.   yes   (no)

2. Laura went to get x-rays.   yes   no

3. The insurance company pays $29.06 for the lab fees.   yes   no

4. Laura pays $29.06 for the lab fees.   yes   no

5. Laura went to the pharmacy on March 10, 2008.   yes   no

6. Laura pays $21.06 for the pharmacy.   yes   no

7. Laura has a question about this paper. She should
   call Williston Health Clinic at 1-800-555-2277.   yes   no

8. Laura can call at 8:30 A.M. on Thursday.   yes   no

Technology Connection: Get Health Insurance Information

WRITE. You can use the Internet to find out information about health insurance companies. Complete the online form for health insurance information.

Insurance Coverage Online

Your Information

ZIP Code: _____   Requested Coverage Date: [/   /]
                                                      (mm/dd/yy)

Person

First name: _____   Gender
                                  ◯ ◯   Date of Birth [/   /]
Last name: _____   M   F   (mm/dd/yy)

Tobacco User

◯ ◯   Height: [ ] feet [ ] inches   Weight: [ ] pounds
Yes No

What is this person's occupation? _____

Spouse

First name: _____   Gender
                                  ◯ ◯   Date of Birth [/   /]
Last name: _____   M   F   (mm/dd/yy)

Tobacco User

◯ ◯   Height: [ ] feet [ ] inches   Weight: [ ] pounds
Yes No

What is this person's occupation? _____

Coverage desired:

◯ Medical   ◯ Dental   ◯ Vision   ◯ Maternity   ◯ Life

Practice Test

LISTENING: Listen to the conversations. Then choose the correct answer for each sentence.

1.
  A. Get well soon.
  B. You should rest.
  C. She has the flu.
  D. No, I'm not. I'm really sick.

2.
  A. You should drink liquids.
  B. I have a headache and a sore throat.
  C. That's too bad.
  D. You shouldn't eat hot foods.

3. Mr. Ruiz is _____ .
  A. at home
  B. at the clinic
  C. at work
  D. at the drugstore

4. His _____ hurts.
  A. throat
  B. head
  C. nose
  D. foot

5. He should _____ and have some juice.
  A. rest
  B. go to work
  C. play
  D. take pain relievers

GRAMMAR AND VOCABULARY: Choose the correct word to complete each sentence.

6. Laura _____ a cough.
  A. is
  B. hurts
  C. has
  D. have

7. Do you _____ a fever?
  A. have
  B. has
  C. feel
  D. hurt

8. We _____ the flu.
  A. are have
  B. don't have
  C. doesn't have
  D. aren't

9. Hector's _____ hurt.
  A. tooth
  B. neck
  C. feet
  D. back

10. Ema's _____ hurts.
  A. hands
  B. feet
  C. head
  D. ears

11. Sam's back hurts. He _____ use a heating pad.
  A. is
  B. should
  C. shouldn't
  D. has

12. Tina has a cold. She _____ drink orange juice.
   A. shouldn't
   B. don't
   C. has
   D. should

13. Fran has a fever. _____ I call 911?
   A. Am
   B. Does
   C. Should
   D. Have

14. My sister has the _____.
   A. flu
   B. runny nose
   C. earache
   D. cold

15. Jerome is _____. He has a sore throat and a fever.
   A. hurts
   B. sick
   C. well
   D. sorry

READING: Look at the medicine label. Choose the correct answer.

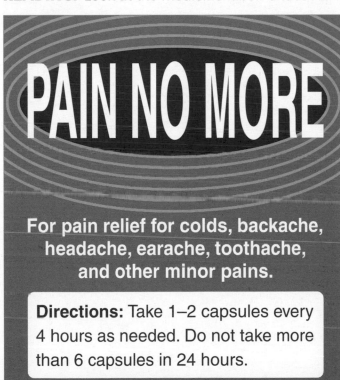

PAIN NO MORE

For pain relief for colds, backache, headache, earache, toothache, and other minor pains.

Directions: Take 1–2 capsules every 4 hours as needed. Do not take more than 6 capsules in 24 hours.

16. Tran has a headache. He takes _____ capsules at 10:00 A.M.
   A. 12
   B. 2
   C. 4
   D. 6

17. Tran should take more medicine at _____.
   A. 1:00 P.M.
   B. 2:00 P.M.
   C. 4:00 P.M.
   D. 12:00 A.M.

18. Pat takes 2 capsules at 9:00 A.M. and 2 more at 2:00 P.M. She takes 1 more at 6:00 P.M. At 10:00 P.M., she should take _____.
   A. 2 capsules
   B. 0 capsules
   C. 1 capsule
   D. 6 capsules

19. "Pain No More" does not help _____.
   A. a backache
   B. an earache
   C. a headache
   D. a cough

20. Greg takes two capsules for his backache at 6:00 P.M. He should take more capsules at _____.
   A. 4:00 P.M.
   B. 8:00 P.M.
   C. 10:00 P.M.
   D. 9:00 P.M.

UNIT 12 Planning Ahead

Lesson 1

1 **WRITE.** Complete the sentences with *is going to* or *are going to*.

1. This weekend, Eduardo _____*is going to*_____ move to a new apartment.

2. Lise and I _____ visit our friends in Montreal.

3. My best friend _____ get married next week.

4. He and his wife _____ go on a honeymoon to Bermuda.

5. My aunt _____ have a baby next month.

6. I _____ buy a car next week.

2 **WRITE.** Complete the sentences. Use the words in the box.

move to a new city	finish school	start my new job
~~ask for a raise~~	rent an apartment	

1. I do good work and should get more money. I'm going to _____*ask for a raise*_____ .

2. I lived in Newark, but now I'm going to Philadelphia to live. I'm going to

   _____ .

3. When I get to Philadelphia, I'm going to _____ .

4. I finish my old job on Thursday, and I'm going to _____
   on Monday.

5. My sister is taking her last three classes now. She is going to _____
   next month.

3 **WRITE** sentences. Put the words in order.

1. going / I / ask / to / am / raise / for / a _____*I am going to ask for a raise.*_____

2. finish / to / school / You / going / aren't / this / year _____

3. city / a / new / We / to / going / are / move / to _____

4. sell / My / their / parents / to / aren't / house / going _____

5. David / computer / is / new / going / a / to / buy _____

6. isn't / look / She / going / for / to / job / a / new _____

Lesson 2

1 CIRCLE. Read the sentences. Circle the correct object pronouns.

1. *A:* Are you going to sell your house? *B:* No, I'm not going to sell **(it)**/ **you**.

2. *A:* Can you call me at 4:00? *B:* Yes, I can call **me / you** then.

3. *A:* Are you inviting Linda? *B:* No, I'm not inviting **her / us**.

4. Ali and Tesia always do the homework. I should ask **them / him** about **it / her**.

5. I'm buying a computer for my brother and me. I'm buying **it / them** for **you / us**.

2 WRITE. Complete the paragraph. Use the correct object pronoun or the correct form of *be going to*. Use the words in parentheses as clues.

Mark has a new friend, Silvia. They (1) ____*are going to go*____ (go) to a movie tonight.

Mark went to the store to buy a new shirt and jacket. He's going to wear (2) _____

(the shirt and jacket) tonight. Silvia (3) _____ (meet) Mark at 6:30.

She's going to wait for (4) _____ (Mark) in front of the theater. I'm going

to meet (5) _____ (Mark and Silvia) after the movie. We

(6) _____ (go) to a Japanese restaurant. I (7) _____

(bring) my sister, too. Silvia knows (8) _____ (my sister) but Mark doesn't.

3 WRITE AND MATCH. Unscramble the letters and write the word on the line. Then match with the activity that is going to happen next.

__*b*__ 1. Rachid is going to sell his
   ____*house*____.
   e h o u s

_____ 2. Fred is going to get
   _____.
   r e d i r a m

_____ 3. Ines is going to _____
   school.   **n i f i h s**

_____ 4. Olivia is going to ask for a
   _____.
   i a s e r

_____ 5. Tomas is going to _____
   a new job.   **r s t a t**

a. Then he's going to go on a
   _____.
   n o o h o n m y e

b. Then he's going to ___*move*___ to
   California.   **v o m e**

c. Then she's going to rent an expensive
   _____.
   p r a t e m a n t

d. Then he's going to ask for a
   _____.
   s i r a e

e. Then she's going to start a new
   _____.
   o b j

Lesson 3

WCD, 45

1 **LISTEN** and circle the pronunciation you hear. Listen again and match the person with the activity.

_f_ 1. I'm (going to) / gonna

_____ 2. I'm not **going to** / **gonna**

_____ 3. Eva's **going to** / **gonna**

_____ 4. She isn't **going to** / **gonna**

_____ 5. My brothers are **going to** / **gonna**

_____ 6. They aren't **going to** / **gonna**

_____ 7. Are you **going to** / **gonna**

_____ 8. Are you **going to** / **gonna**

a. move to Seattle.

b. sell the house.

c. look for a new job?

d. make pizza.

e. prepare some Chinese food.

f. work tonight.

g. watch TV.

h. ask for a raise?

2 **MATCH** the questions and answers.

_c_ 1. Do you have any plans for the weekend?

_____ 2. What are you doing tomorrow?

_____ 3. Are you doing anything special next Tuesday?

_____ 4. What is Alice doing this weekend?

_____ 5. What are Ken and Brenda doing tomorrow?

_____ 6. Do you and Victor have any plans for the weekend?

a. They're going to study in the library.

b. We're going to fix the car on Saturday.

c. I'm going to play soccer on Saturday.

d. She's going to help her friend move.

e. I'm going to visit my aunt tomorrow.

f. I don't have any plans for Tuesday.

3 **READ** and arrange the conversation in order. Write the numbers.

_____ B: Sure! What time should I be there?

_____ A: Well, …. I'm going to paint the apartment in the afternoon. Can you give me a hand?

_1_ A: What are you doing this weekend?

_____ B: Great. See you then.

_____ B: I'm going to go shopping Saturday morning. Why?

_____ A: How about 1:00?

Culture and Communication — *Talk about Your Plans*

1 WRITE. Complete the conversation. Use the phrases in the box.

I'm going to	Are you going to	What time
You're going to	It's my favorite	~~what are you going to~~

Ben: Hi, Julia. Say, (1) _what are you going to_
       do this weekend?

Julia: On Saturday, (2) _____
        play football.

Ben: What? (3) _____ play
        football?

Julia: Well, sure. Girls can play football, too!

        (4) _____ sport!

Ben: I didn't know that.

        (5) _____ are you
        going to play?

Julia: The game is going to start at 10:00. (6) _____ come?

Ben: I'll try.

2 READ the conversation. Then practice with a partner.

A: What are you going to do this weekend?

B: I'm going to go to a museum. Do you want to come?

A: No thanks. I'm going to paint the cabinets in the bathroom.

B: That doesn't sound like much fun.

A: I really like it!

Useful Expressions

Ways to talk about plans

That sounds like fun.

That doesn't sound like much fun.

That's a good idea.

That sounds boring.

Lesson 4

1 **WRITE.** Complete the sentences. Use the phrases in the box.

fix the bed	call the phone company	get cable television	~~get Internet access~~
vacuum the carpet	put in a new microwave	fix the dishwasher	buy a new refrigerator

1. I want to read my email at home. I'm going to _____ get Internet access _____.

2. Cameron wants to watch his favorite TV programs. He's going to _____.

3. Alex wants to change her phone plan. She's going to _____.

4. Felipe's friends are going to sleep at his house next week. He's going to _____.

5. Maria has a lot of dishes to wash. She's going to _____.

6. Henri wants to cook his food fast. He's going to _____.

7. Tran can't keep his food cold. He's going to _____.

8. Some friends are going to visit Alicia, and she wants the floor to be clean. She's going to

_____

2 **LOOK AND WRITE.** Look at the "TO DO" list. Then write answers to the questions.

TO DO			
When?	**Alicia**	**Bill**	**Felipe and Henri**
Saturday morning	clean the kitchen	go shopping	clean the refrigerator
Saturday afternoon	fix the door	prepare dinner	wash the windows
Saturday night	paint the door	fix the computer	study

1. Is Alicia going to clean the kitchen Saturday morning? _Yes, she is._

2. Is she going to go shopping Saturday morning? _No, she's not._

3. Is Bill going to go shopping Saturday? _____

4. Is he going to study Saturday night? _____

5. Are Felipe and Henri going to wash the windows in the afternoon? _____

6. Are they going to paint the door Saturday night? _____

7. Is Alicia going to prepare dinner Saturday afternoon? _____

8. Are Felipe and Henri going to study Saturday night? _____

3 WRITE. Complete the questions and answers. Use *is going to* and *are going to* in the questions.

1. __Is__ Maya __going to__ move to a new apartment? Yes, __she is__ .

2. _____ the landlord _____ paint the apartment? No, _____ .

3. _____ Maya's friends _____ help her move? Yes, _____ .

4. _____ you _____ fix the car this weekend? No, _____ .

5. _____ you and Jack _____ clean the apartment this weekend? No, _____ .

6. _____ Cody _____ fix the windows? Yes, _____ .

4 WHAT ABOUT YOU? Write sentences using *going to*. Tell if you are going to do the activities next week.

1. (study) _I'm going to study for a test._ or _I'm not going to study for a test._

2. (ask for a raise) _____

3. (move to a new city) _____

4. (look for a new job) _____

5. (go to the movies) _____

6. (clean the house/apartment) _____

5 READ AND WRITE. In Pepe's family, everyone is going to be working at home this weekend. Read about what they are going to do. Then complete the sentences. Use the words in the box.

the bedroom	~~the garage~~	the yard
the living room	the bathroom	the kitchen

1. Al's going to fix his bicycle and wash the car. He's going to be in ____the garage____ .

2. Helen is going to vacuum the carpet and clean the furniture. She's going to dust the shelves and organize the magazines and books on the shelves. She's going to be in _____ .

3. Olga is going to fix the water pipes in the shower. She's going to clean the toilet and floor, too. Olga is going to work in _____ .

4. Karl is going to put the food away in the refrigerator and wash the dishes. Then he's going to prepare a fruit salad. He's going to be in _____ .

5. Pepe is going to fix his bed and paint the dresser. He's going to fix his closet door. He's going to work in _____ .

6. Emma is going to get some flowers and vegetables from the garden. She's also going to cut the grass. She's going to be in _____ .

Family Connection — *Things That Use Electricity*

1 **LOOK AND WRITE.** Look at the household appliances. Write the names. Use the words in the box.

stove	microwave oven	~~refrigerator~~	toaster
vacuum cleaner	washer	dryer	iron

1

refrigerator

2

_____

3

_____

4

_____

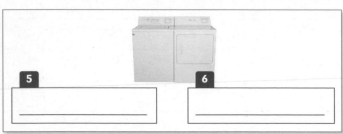

5   **6**

_____   _____

7

_____

8

_____

2 **READ AND WRITE.** There was a storm. The electricity doesn't work. Nick calls the electric company. Complete the conversation. Use the words in the box.

your account number	~~I'm calling~~	the electricity
with the wires	your name and address	What time

Electric Co.: Central Electric Company. How can I help you?

Nick: (1) _____ I'm calling _____ because (2) _____ is out.

Electric Co: What's (3) _____, please?

Nick: It's Nick Tremont at 492 Maple Street.

Electric Co: What's (4) _____?

Nick: 432115003951.

Electric Co: OK. I see there is a problem (5) _____ in your neighborhood. Some workers are there now.

Nick: (6) _____ are we going to get electricity again?

Electric Co: The electricity is going to be back on by 8:00 this evening.

Nick: OK. Thank you.

3 LOOK AND CIRCLE. Look at Nick's electric bill. Circle these things on the bill.

~~his name~~	Nick's address	the account number
the amount to pay	the date he needs to pay	the name of the company

---

Central Electric Co
P.O. Box 567
Atlanta, GA 30301

Billing Date
JUN 26, 2009

Account Number
432115003951

Pay this Amount
$57.53

(Nicolas Tremont)
492 Maple Street
Decatur, GA 30030

Rate	Previous Reading	Present Reading	Units Unit Cost	Amount
Residential	96420	96943	523 x $.11/kwh	57.53

Payable upon receipt. Please pay your current month charges before 07/27/09.

Customer Information: **800 555 2877**   To Report a Power Outage: **800 555 2300**

---

4 CIRCLE *yes* or *no*.

1. The electric company is at 492 Maple Street.   yes   (no)

2. Nick pays $57.23.   yes   no

3. Nick should pay the bill before August 26, 2009.   yes   no

4. For questions about his electric bill, Nick calls: (800) 555-2877.   yes   no

5. When the electricity goes out, Nick calls (800) 555-2877.   yes   no

5 REAL-LIFE LESSON. Ask a family member about household appliances and items that use electricity. Make a list of them.

Appliance or Item	Where is it? (What room)	How many?
air conditioner		

Community Connection — *Shop for Appliances*

1 **READ** the conversation.

Flora: Excuse me. I'm looking for a new washer. Could you answer some questions for me?

Salesclerk: Sure. We have several different **models** to choose from.

Flora: I see. What's special about the **energy-efficient** model?

Salesclerk: **Energy-efficient** means that it doesn't use much electricity. The machine works the same, but it's going to save you money on your electricity bill. The energy-efficient machine costs more than the normal washer.

Flora: Is there a **guarantee** or **warranty** with it?

Salesclerk: Yes. There's a 6-month **guarantee**. There's also a **warranty** for 12 months. We fix broken machines at no charge for a year.

Flora: That's good.

Salesclerk: Don't lose your receipt.

Flora: Can I **install** the washer or do I call a plumber to connect it?

Salesclerk: The instructions for installing and using the washer are in the owner's **manual**.

Flora: Well, thanks for your help. I'm going to think about this and talk with my family about it.

Salesclerk: OK. Let me know what you decide.

---

energy-efficient doesn't use a lot of electricity (or other form of power)

guarantee a promise that something is going to work

install to put in place and connect an appliance so you can use it

model a style or type

owner's manual a small book that tells you how to use an appliance or machine

warranty a written promise to fix an appliance if it doesn't work

---

2 **WRITE** answers to the questions.

1. What appliance is Flora looking for? *She is looking for a washer.*

2. Which model is going to save money on Flora's electric bill? _____

3. Which model costs more in the store? _____

4. How long is the guarantee? _____

5. How long is the warranty? _____

6. Where are the instructions for the machine? _____

3 WRITE. Complete the warranty card. Use your own information and the information on the receipt.

A1Appliances Limited Warranty Program

All products from A-One Appliances must be registered within 10 days of purchase to start this warranty.
Mail the complete registration form, along with a copy of the original sales receipt, to:

Warranty Registration A-One Appliances
5682 North Street, St. Louis, MO 63166

Name _____

Street Address _____

City _____ State _____ Zip Code _____ Phone _____

Item Purchased _____ Date of Purchase _____

Store Where Purchased _____ Model # _____

Super Price Appliances

262 Lakeview Road   Erie, PA

```
03/30/09
Model #    Item            Unit Price
952061     Heavy-duty        $495.95
           Energy-efficient
           washer


           TOTAL             $495.95
```

4 REAL-LIFE LESSON. Ask a friend or neighbor about household appliances. Use the questions below or your own questions.

1. Where do you shop for appliances?	
2. Did you buy any appliances last year?	
3. Did you use the guarantee or warranty on an item?	
4. What do you do when an appliance breaks or doesn't work?	
5. Are you planning to buy any appliances this year?	
6. What do you look for before you buy an appliance?	

Career Connection — *Career and Personal Goals*

1 **READ AND WRITE.** Read and complete the conversation. Use the words in the box.

I can buy	~~You're going to~~	it's going
are you going to	I should take	I'm going to

> *Leyla:* Wow, Isabel! That's so great. (1) *You're going to* finish school next month. What (2) _____ do after that?
>
> *Isabel:* Laura just gave me some information about a job opening. (3) _____ apply for that, I think.
>
> *Leyla:* Does it pay better?
>
> *Isabel:* Yes, it does. Plus, (4) _____ be more responsibility, so it will be more interesting for me.
>
> *Leyla:* So what other plans do you have?
>
> *Isabel:* Well, now that I don't have to pay for classes, maybe (5) _____ a new dryer. Ours isn't working very well right now. What about you?
>
> *Leyla:* I'm not sure. Maybe (6) _____ some classes sometime.
>
> *Isabel:* I think you should.

2 **WRITE** answers to the questions.

1. Is Isabel going to finish school next month? _____

2. Is Laura going to apply for a new job? _____

3. Does the new job pay the same money? _____

4. Does Isabel need to pay for classes now? _____

5. What is Isabel going to buy? _____

6. Is Leyla applying for a new job? _____

7. What is Leyla planning to do sometime? _____

3 **WHAT ABOUT YOU?** Think about your goals. Complete the chart about your goals. Use the goals in Activity 3 or your own plans.

Personal Goals	Educational Goals	Workplace Goals

Technology Connection: Online Banking

4 **LOOK AND WRITE.** Look at the computer screen. Isabel is going to pay her bills online. Answer the questions about it.

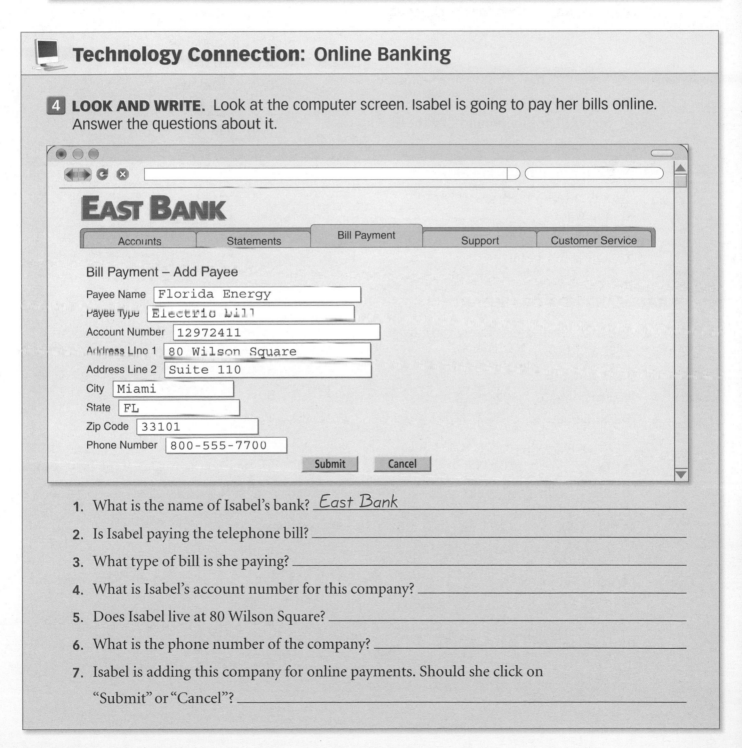

EAST BANK

| Accounts | Statements | Bill Payment | Support | Customer Service |

Bill Payment – Add Payee

Payee Name: Florida Energy
Payee Type: Electric bill
Account Number: 12972411
Address Line 1: 80 Wilson Square
Address Line 2: Suite 110
City: Miami
State: FL
Zip Code: 33101
Phone Number: 800-555-7700

Submit   Cancel

1. What is the name of Isabel's bank? *East Bank*

2. Is Isabel paying the telephone bill? _____

3. What type of bill is she paying? _____

4. What is Isabel's account number for this company? _____

5. Does Isabel live at 80 Wilson Square? _____

6. What is the phone number of the company? _____

7. Isabel is adding this company for online payments. Should she click on "Submit" or "Cancel"? _____

Unit 12 Test

LISTENING: Listen to the conversations. Then choose the correct answer for each sentence.

1.
   A. Sorry, I can't this weekend.
   B. Sure!
   C. They're going to go on their honeymoon.
   D. I'm going to clean the apartment on Saturday morning.

2.
   A. I'm going to wash my car on Sunday.
   B. Kim is going to go shopping.
   C. Sure! What time should I be there?
   D. Yes, I am.

3. What is he going to look for tomorrow?
   A. a new apartment
   B. a new job
   C. a new car
   D. a new computer

4. She's going to work on _____.
   A. her car
   B. her apartment
   C. the house
   D. the floors

5. She's going to fix _____.
   A. the doors
   B. the windows
   C. the toilet
   D. the lights

GRAMMAR AND VOCABULARY: Choose the correct word to complete each sentence.

6. Jim _____ buy a new microwave oven.
   A. am going to
   B. is going to
   C. are going to
   D. going to

7. _____ you going to ask for a raise?
   A. Is
   B. Am
   C. Was
   D. Are

8. Greg and Al _____ take a class next year.
   A. aren't going to
   B. is going to
   C. am not going to
   D. isn't going to

9. Is Ken going to move next month?
   No, he _____.
   A. isn't
   B. is
   C. aren't
   D. are not

10. Marie is going to _____ the light tomorrow.
   A. fixing
   B. fixed
   C. fix
   D. fixes

11. We _____ going to study this weekend.
   A. didn't
   B. don't
   C. can't
   D. aren't

12. Is George inviting Pam and Ella?
Yes, he's inviting _____.
A. it
B. them
C. her
D. us

13. Did you call Ms. Jones?
Yes, I called _____.
A. her
B. him
C. you
D. it

14. Is Ines going to the movies with you and me?
Yes, she's going with _____.
A. you
B. them
C. us
D. me

15. Li is sending a package to _____.
A. I
B. me
C. she
D. they

READING: Read. Then choose the correct answer.

		Payment Due 12/12/09	Amount Due $73.51

Central Telephone Co
P.O. Box 567
Atlanta, GA 30301

Nicolas Tremont
492 Maple Street
Decatur, GA 30030

Account Number: 115003431
Bill Date: NOV 12, 2009

Previous Bill	Payments	Charges	Amount Due
$86.13	$86.13	$73.51	$73.51

TOTAL DUE: Please pay this amount: $73.51

16. This is _____.
A. an electric bill
B. a telephone bill
C. a shopping receipt
D. bank statement

17. _____ should pay the bill.
A. Central Telephone
B. Bill Date
C. Nicolas Tremont
D. Decatur

18. He should pay _____.
A. $73.51
B. $86.13
C. $4.92
D. $12.09

19. He should pay before _____.
A. November 12
B. December 12
C. June 12
D. January 12

20. How much did he pay last month?
A. $73.51
B. $11.50
C. $86.13
D. $300.30

Correlation Table

Student Book	Workbook
Pre-Unit	
2–5	2–5
Unit 1	
6–7	6
8–9	7
10–11	8–9
12–13	10
14–15	11
16–17	12–13
18–19	14–15
20	16–17
21	18–19
Unit 2	
22–23	20
24–25	21
26–27	22–23
28–29	24
30–31	25
32–33	26–27
34–35	28–29
36	30–31
37	32–33
Unit 3	
38–39	34
40–41	35
42–43	36–37
44–45	38
46–47	39
48–49	40–41
50–51	42–43
52	44–45
53	46–47
Unit 4	
54–55	48
56–57	49
58–59	50–51
60–61	52
62–63	53
64–65	54–55
66–67	56–57
68	58–59
69	60–61

Student Book	Workbook
Unit 5	
70–71	62
72–73	63
74–75	64–65
76–77	66
78–79	67
80–81	68–69
82–83	70–71
84	72–73
85	74–75
Unit 6	
86–87	76
88–89	77
90–91	78–79
92–93	80
94–95	81
96–97	82–83
98–99	84–85
100	86–87
101	88–89
Unit 7	
102–103	90
104–105	91
106–107	92–93
108–109	94
110–111	95
112–113	96–97
114–115	98–99
116	100–101
117	102–103
Unit 8	
118–119	104
120–121	105
122–123	106–107
124–125	108
126–127	109
128–129	110–111
130–131	112–113
132	114–115
133	116–117

Student Book	Workbook
Unit 9	
134–135	118
136–137	119
138–139	120–121
140–141	122
142–143	123
144–145	124–125
146–147	126–127
148	128–129
149	130–131
Unit 10	
150–151	132
152–153	133
154–155	134–135
156–157	136
158–159	137
160–161	138–139
162–163	140–141
164	142–143
165	144–145
Unit 11	
166–167	146
168–169	147
170–171	148–149
172–173	150
174–175	151
176–177	152–153
178–179	154–155
180	156–157
181	158–159
Unit 12	
182–183	160
184–185	161
186–187	162–163
188–189	164
190–191	165
192–193	166–167
194–195	168–169
196	170–171
197	172–173